PRAISE FOR
RETURN TO THE GARDEN

Get ready for a fascinating story to grip your heart! Rebecca Mann Kelly has written a powerful book about how God will deliver you from abuse, shame, rejection, and self-condemnation. *Return to the Garden* is a healing journey of *Discovering God's Original Design for Women*. You will be touched deeply by God's grace moving through this author's difficult past. I found myself applauding Rebecca more than once for her heartfelt honesty. This book will set many free from feeling like the enemy has them wrapped up in despair and discouragement. The pain of your past will evaporate and a new grace will fill your heart to live as God has designed you to live as His daughter, His royal daughter. Read it and be set free! Be sure to buy an extra copy for a friend, they will thank you for it!

Dr. Brian Simmons, Passion & Fire Ministries, lead translator of *The Passion Translation*

Turning your unhealed pain into your greatest strength is the story of the author, Rebecca Mann Kelly. *Return to the Garden* speaks of a freedom journey that removes the shackles of guilt, shame, and religion. My prayer is that this book will bring wholeness to all of his daughters as they experience the truth of God's character and the beauty of His love.

Dr. Leif Hetland, President and Founder of Global Mission Awareness, Author of *Called to Reign* and *Healing the Orphan Spirit*

There is no greater time in history for Rebecca Mann Kelly to tell her story, confront archaic lies, and release God's incredible revelation than right now. Through the poignant telling of her own journey, Rebecca invites the reader to delve into a pure understanding of God's intentional design for women, and relational design for men and women. *Return To The Garden* will bring transformative truth and powerful identity to anyone who reads it. Through her scriptural foundations, Rebecca lays a roadmap for the reader to step into healing and hope found through the word of God. Through her unique questions, Rebecca helps both men and women unwind years of accepted behavior and beliefs. This book is a must for women who have lost their voice, ignored their emotions, and grown numb in their relationships - and are ready to heal. This book is a must for any couple that is struggling to understand each other, and feels like they are missing the Godly truth of what marriage should be. This book is a must for any leader who understands the need for women to operate in their God ordained calling and function. Without a doubt, this book will take you to a true place of identity, love, and authority!

Annie Byrne, Lead Pastor, Kingdom Culture Church

From a soft, open, and deep place in her heart, Rebecca Mann Kelly has bravely released her story in all its pain and joy; darkness and light; captivity and freedom. *Return to the Garden* delivers a roadmap to breakthrough for any woman living under relationship oppression. Rebecca defines Christian feminism afresh as the original design for men and women as equals. This truth has been distorted far too long. I commend this woman of courage and pray her true story will set many sisters free.

Christine Tracy, Author of *Tapestry - The Divine Design for Your Life*

We all have the choice to step out of captivity and walk in the abundant life Jesus gave us when He broke the curse. Rebecca Mann Kelly shares how God set her free from a life of people pleasing, control, religion, shame and emotional abuse. She leads the reader out of being a victim into an overcomer by using truth from God's word, powerful anointed prayers and questions to ask the Holy

Spirit. While reading, every person will encounter the Holy Spirit and learn how uniquely valuable they are. This powerful book gives us the tools to live a life of freedom and intimacy with God like He intended for us in the garden.

Tami Hichman, entrepreneur

The God of our breakthroughs is the same God in our breakdowns. In *Return to the Garden - Discovering God's Original Design for Women*, we see the handprints of the Great Potter who has beautifully formed a masterpiece in and through pain, rejection, religion and abuse with His unconditional love as a Father. We see God's passion to awaken true identity, value, design and destiny of women through the life of the author. Rebecca Mann Kelly wrote with such honesty, courage and conviction as a person who has found freedom and deliverance from cycles and entanglements of control, manipulation, fear, and emotional trauma. Out of the ashes of shame, she arose and found precious nuggets of Truth from the Word-revelations that sustained and armed her through her struggles. Certainly, these life-giving words will greatly empower and awaken women from all races and status to find their design and true identity in God.

The heart and face of God that Rebecca found in her time of brokenness is the same heart and face that she has boldly and passionately expressed in the pages of this book. A clarion call, a voice of hope to the women who are trapped and lost needing to find their own voice and value in the world and within the church.

Jesus came to restore everything back to God's original intent. The Apostle Paul wrote, "There is neither Jew nor Gentile, neither slave nor free, nor is there male and female, for you are all one in Christ Jesus" (Galatians 3:28). This book compels everyone to reconsider how we view and value the women who are image-bearers of God as much as the men. More than ever, it is time to see them through the eyes of the Father with great love, honor and respect.

It is a privilege to have known the author. Together with my wife Ahlmira, we celebrate her and the freedom that she has found in God. I highly recommend this book not just to the women who are going through relational struggles but to all the men who are humble enough and willing to take time to truly understand God's heart for the women.

Paul Yadao, Senior Pastor, Destiny Ministries International, Philippines

Return to the Garden offers women important insights into the emotional, relational and spiritual growth process that even the most challenging marriages can provide. Rebecca offers the story of her own journey, while at the same time providing guidance for how the reader can apply scripturally based applications to their own lives. Each chapter contains reflections on Biblical premises, along with questions for the reader to consider. Read alone, or as part of a group study, this book will assist you in learning more about yourself and, more importantly, about God's desire for you to live an authentic life as the woman He created you to be.

Melody Bacon, PhD, Psychologist and Author

God has equipped Rebecca- through her vulnerable and honest testimony- to be the ultimate spirit-filled whistle-blower for any woman who suspects she might be living in marital bondage - diminished, silenced and controlled by the ungodly beliefs and actions of her spouse, captive to the expectations and obligations of religion that keep her stuck in the system of "right-doing." Filled with hope and trust in a really adoring, intimate, and powerful God, Rebecca offers a gentle and clear invitation to ask for more: to pursue and experience the freedom, confidence and abundant life He designed, intended and purchased for each and every woman.

Ashley Camozzi, friend of the author

This powerful testimony will surely bring freedom to many women trapped in secret abuse, manipulation, and control. Rebecca's vulnerability, practical questions, and prayers will help you release fear and trauma in Jesus's name. Are you in a controlling relationship and need courage? This book can empower you to move into the safe arms of the one who created you, the one that walked with us initially.

It's time to discover how relationships are supposed to be and return to the garden and God's original design.

Cathy Greer, Founder, Kingdom Women International & Mission Support Network

The message and revelation Rebecca Kelly delivers in *Return to the Garden* is powerful, relevant, and absolutely vital. With every page, I found myself cheering in agreement as Rebecca champions the relationships and roles God intended for His daughters and provides guidance on how to get back to it. Rebecca shares Biblical insight on the relational dynamic between men and women, told beautifully and vulnerably through her testimony of living asleep and awakening to truth, healing, and freedom. Though Rebecca's story may be different than yours, the trials, truth and victory in it are universally relatable. Every woman - and man - can receive profound wisdom and encouragement from *Return to the Garden*.

Erin Stone, Freelance Writer

Powerful . . . Transparent . . . Authentic . . . Rebecca Mann Kelly has earned the authority to speak into the lives of so many women who have been abused by religion and the religious structure. She is a true "overcomer" who is embracing the fullness of her spiritual inheritance and intimate relationship as a daughter of the King. "He who overcomes shall inherit all things, and I will be his God and he shall be My son" (Revelation 21:7, NKJV). This deeply riveting story reveals how God works with us to break through the lies of the enemy coming from those who operate in influence and authority in our lives. As Rebecca chose to seek the truth directly from the Lord, she was healed, delivered, and set free to know her true identity in Christ which is the foundation to understanding our spiritual inheritance. She also discovered her true honored position as a daughter of the King by establishing a deep intimacy during this process. *Return to the Garden* brings hope to everyone who has been stuck in lies that keep so many in bondage.

Pastor Linda Sloan, Life Coach, Deliverance Minister

Return to the Garden contains profound insight that God's original plan for women does not include forced or default subservience. This moving personal story of overcoming not only acts as a survival guide, but reminds us of the God-given freedom that women are meant to live in.

Dr. Michelle Lupica, D.O.

Rebecca gives a raw and real look at what it means to walk as a daughter created by God. The way she weaves her testimony and healing through the chapters of this book will keep you devoured in its pages. Rebecca will help you understand the heart of Jesus while bringing you back to His feet. I could not recommend this book more.

Alissa Circle, Author of (Be) Known Bible study and founder of Be Together Co.

Return to the Garden is a powerful book that will move you and invite you into deeper understanding and challenge the destructive mindsets that may be within you. I believe this book will not only bring women out of oppression, but it will also awaken men and the body of Christ to what God's original design for mankind truly was. Rebecca is, without question, an example of a woman who is fully surrendered to God and fully walking in the authority and calling that God has placed on her. I have no doubt that her words will bring wholeness and healing to those who allow the Holy Spirit to illuminate the true heart of God towards His children.

Mya Lazaro, kingdom mom, wife and businesswoman

Return to the Garden is absolutely stunning. Rebecca's beautiful autobiographical story is interwoven with biblical, foundational theology of women and men, and had my full attention from start to finish. For far too long, women have been trapped under the lies of people-pleasing religiosity and deferring their God-ordained authority to others in an effort to appear humble. Rebecca reminds her readers that the original design of God is for woman and man to co-rule, co-reign, co-labor, and co-create. Over the course of the book, Rebecca utilizes the vulnerability of her own stories and prophetic encounters with God to empower other women to step whole-heartedly into all that God has intended for them. This is an absolute must-read for every single woman (and man!) in the Church and I cannot recommend this book any higher!

Kate Hodges, M.Div., Worship Leader, Songwriter

Return to the Garden is a powerful testimony of how the freedom Jesus purchased for us on the cross actually transforms us from the inside out, and has the power to save us. No pit is so deep that God's love cannot meet us, lead us to Himself and restore our value and identity. Rebecca so beautifully and vulnerably unpacks her journey, inviting us every step of the way into new levels of freedom. No matter where you find yourself, this book will challenge, encourage and propel you into greater levels of trust, understanding and your worth in Jesus.

Pastor Melanie Foust, Oceans Church

Stories of God's uncanny ability to restore and redeem always lead us to a deeper love for Jesus. Rebecca Mann Kelly is one of those real-life testaments of God's goodness and grace. Rebecca's journey will touch your heart and her relationship with The Holy Spirit will inspire your faith. Many will be blessed by her testimony and her message.

Mark & Rachelle Francey, Lead Pastors, Oceans Church

This book is an authentic and vulnerable journey of a woman pursuing a life of faith without compromise or reservations. Her tenacity in searching for healing and forgiveness with God and others inspires hope. Rebecca shows great courage in the beautiful unfolding of her story and weaves together God's original design and heart for all His daughters. The joy and healing that comes from walking out her trauma with the Holy Spirit's guidance is desperately needed for any woman struggling from self-worth, abuse and knowing her identity in God.

Lisa C. Shirvanian-Wolfe, MFT, Certified Spiritual Dir. and **Paul A. Wolfe,** MBA, MA Philosophy of Religion

RETURN TO THE GARDEN

RETURN TO THE GARDEN

*Discovering God's Original
Design for Women*

REBECCA MANN KELLY

Copyright © 2023 by Rebecca Mann Kelly

ISBN Hardcover: 979-8-88739-021-5
ISBN Softcover: 979-8-88739-020-8
ISBN Ebook: 979-8-88739-022-2

All rights reserved. No part of this book may be reproduced or transmitted in any form or by any means, electronic or mechanical, including photocopying, recording or by any information storage and retrieval system, without permission in writing from the copyright owner. For information on distribution rights, royalties, derivative works or licensing opportunities on behalf of this content or work, please contact the publisher at the address below.

Although the author and publisher have made every effort to ensure that the information and advice in this book were correct and accurate at press time, the author and publisher do not assume and hereby disclaim any liability to any party for any loss, damage, or disruption caused from acting upon the information in this book or by errors or omissions, whether such errors or omissions result from negligence, accident, or any other cause.

Printed in the United States of America.

For you, Dad. When God told you that you would have two daughters (and not sons), you celebrated. I always knew how much you loved me. I could feel it in your hugs and in your tenderness. You were always proud of me, and you always believed in me. You didn't have to try hard to care for me. It was never a task or a burden. You're why I knew something was really wrong in my relationships. Thanks for being the example that tethered me to hope.

TABLE OF CONTENTS

Prologue .... *xvii*

PART I

Chapter One: The Day I Woke Up 3

Chapter Two: Returning to the Garden 11

Chapter Three: Into Captivity 23

Chapter Four: Great Awakening 39

Chapter Five: Back into Bondage 53

Chapter Six: Living in the Curse: Emotional Abuse
and Narcissism 71

PART II

Chapter Seven: Removing the Yoke......................... 99

Chapter Eight: Stepping Out of the Curse................. 111

Chapter Nine: Free Indeed 133

Chapter Ten: Christian Feminism 159

Chapter Eleven: Hidden Pain and Learning to Feel Again 181

Conclusion 193

Epilogue *201*

About the Author: *205*

PROLOGUE

Your mission is to open blind eyes, to set prisoners free from dark dwellings, and to open prison doors to those who are held by darkness...But this is a people plundered and robbed, trapped in holes and hidden in houses of bondage. They are like prey that no one will rescue, like spoil with no one to say, "Bring them back!" Doesn't anyone understand this? Will any of you pay attention to this in the future?

Isaiah 42: 7, 22-23 (TPT)

We're in the large, open kitchen and living room area of our beautiful California home. There's a Bible study going on, and everyone is sitting in chairs and couches in a big circle—about fifteen people.

From my vantage point in the dream, I am behind someone who looks really sick. Extremely thin, she has lost her hair and is hooked up to all these wires and life support tanks. I can't see her face, but it seems like she loses consciousness. I see her head dip into a tray of liquid on her lap. Her mouth and nose submerge in the liquid, and she doesn't wake up.

Everyone continues with the Bible study. No one notices the woman is deathly ill and drowning. And she doesn't seem to notice she's drowning, either. None of the Christians at this meeting are going to rescue her.

I wake up shaken. This was a very vivid dream—one of the most intense I've ever had. I hear these words in my heart: "You do not perceive the dead and dying in your own midst." I have no idea why God would be telling me this. We don't have a Bible study at our house. Who was dead and dying? It didn't make any sense.

I tell my husband Kevin about the dream the next day as we drove home from our out-of-town ski trip. His immediate response is disgust, and he asks me to stop sharing. He is so angry, he doesn't speak to me for the next several hours of driving. I don't know why he's so upset. I don't ask because when I do, he tells me when I ask about his moods, I make them worse. So I stay silent. Our two kids in the back seat stay silent, too.

Several weeks later, I realize who the woman is. I am the drowning, dying woman. I am bald, thin, on life support, unconscious, with my head underwater. I am about to quietly drown in the middle of a Bible study in my own house, and no one notices, not even me. No one sees I am a captive in my own life, and I'm going to die this way.

Everyone thinks we are a happy and successful couple, but I know better. We aren't a couple. Instead, we are two people living in the same house, sharing a bed, with two little kids.

I disconnected my heart from my mind and body a long time ago, but I can still feel it bleeding. I try to ignore it, because I have a strong will. But the pain of my hemorrhaging heart is dull, constant, and unbearable.

I have had two cocktails every night for the past five years. I don't know how I would get through each day without them. Every once in a while, I stop the cocktails for a week just to remind myself that I am not an alcoholic. But I want to fall asleep each night without feeling this pain and suffering. I am afraid of what I will see if I stop to look at myself and what I am becoming.

My life orbits around a man with whom I made a marriage covenant. In my marriage vows, I promised to never consider divorcing. I was already divorced once, and some friends shamed me, calling me a sinner, saying I had let them down. They projected the shame of a belief system that quotes a lot of scripture about how divorce is not Biblical, so never, ever, do it. And I agree, divorce is bad. So I am true to my promise, and I never consider divorce. It's been nine years, I am thirty-eight years old, and I have no choices.

I don't much care for the person I am now. I still remember the Lord, and how I found him after a life of dry religion. I remember how I heard his voice and felt his power, how I saw his signs and wonders. I don't think he's the problem…I feel like I am.

Sometimes when I walk in the hills behind my house, I hear him still. He says I am going to walk through fire. He says he will give me a new wineskin to carry new wine. He says the winter does not last forever but the seed must first fall to the ground and die before it can grow, blossom, and multiply in the spring. He is there when I call, telling me it will be hard, that I am not alone. But it's already hard, and the winter seems eternal. I feel utterly alone.

Part I

Chapter One

THE DAY I WOKE UP

The Spirit of the Lord is upon me, because he has anointed me to preach the gospel to the poor; he has sent me to heal the brokenhearted, to proclaim liberty to the captives and recovery of sight to the blind, to set at liberty those who are oppressed; to proclaim the acceptable year of the Lord. – Jesus

Luke 4:18-19 (NKJV)

ARE YOU OKAY?

We had been married for nine and a half years. I had just had the vivid dream about being thin, bald, on life support, and drowning in my own house in the middle of a Bible study. I hadn't yet realized the dream was about me.

Kevin made me promise to not be gone longer than an hour. I was going to meet my girlfriend Claire for coffee. He didn't want to "watch" the kids longer than that. I didn't have many friends, partly because of Kevin's restrictions, but also because authentic, personal connections were a challenge for me. My heart was surrounded by a giant numbing wall of ice. I had extremely limited emotional capacity for others.

At coffee with Claire, I felt pressured to hurry up and not be late getting home. I was surprised when the conversation took an unexpected turn. Claire said, "I want to ask you a question. Are you okay? My husband and I have noticed how Kevin talks to you sometimes."

I have no idea what possessed me that day to answer her how I did. Claire was not the first person to bring this up—to ask me if how Kevin treated me bothered me. But every time before this, I had defended him, insisted his cruelty was just part of his sarcastic personality, and played it off as if I wasn't upset about it. Honestly, in my own heart and mind, I didn't even know I *was* upset about it. I had been lying to myself about it for a long time. But the truth I've learned about hidden heart pain is this: even if it is stuffed down and far away where it's ignored and denied, no hidden well of pain can stay stuffed away forever. Your pain will eventually have its day.

I surprised myself when I said to Claire, "Can I tell you a secret? I haven't kissed Kevin on the mouth in a long time. When I do, I feel like I'm going to vomit. My entire body screams 'no!' I think there's something really wrong with me."

I couldn't believe I said that out loud. I didn't even remember thinking about it before. It's like it came out of my mouth before I could stop it. But it was true. When Kevin tried to kiss me, I felt like I wanted to die. Of course, I still did my "duty" in the bedroom, because if Kevin wasn't satisfied in that department, it always came back to punish me in the form of his increased moodiness. I was programmed to do anything to avoid the pain of his mistreatment. But despite what I allowed to happen with my body, my mouth would not cooperate. I felt really messed up.

Claire didn't even hesitate when she replied, "You almost vomit when he kisses you because it's the same mouth he uses to talk to you like that."

My jaw dropped, and I sat in stunned silence. At that moment, something like a giant dam broke wide open in my heart. It felt like Claire had fired a missile into my protective shell, waking me up from a really long sleep. Down to my very core, I knew what she said was true. And the thing that shattered inside was this: the lie that the problems with Kevin were all my fault. The lie that I couldn't kiss Kevin on the mouth because something was wrong with me. It was because of him and how he treated me, how he spoke to me.

It's hard to express how deep and monumental this revelation was for me that day. It was the first time in a very long time that I had let something penetrate my heart with truth and light. I had spent nearly a decade trying to be a Godly wife, praying for Kevin, turning the other cheek, putting myself aside, and tiptoeing around Kevin so he would not get triggered and turn his hostility toward me. Perhaps worst of all, I tried to remain small, silent, and compliant so Kevin would never feel insecure, so he could continue to feel powerful and important, so he wouldn't punish me.

But the funny thing is: I really believed I had no choice in the matter, which is why I had never entertained anyone's feedback about Kevin's treatment. I had nowhere to put the feedback, no way to reconcile the dissonance. At my then-pastor's encouragement, I had vowed at my wedding to "never consider a divorce," so I didn't. The enemy had me convinced I had no choice but to endure it. I didn't understand back then that God designed us to always have choices. If he wanted religious robots, he wouldn't have given us free will.

CHAPTER ONE: THE DAY I WOKE UP

Here's the tricky part. Praying for your spouse, turning the other cheek, and putting yourself aside are very Godly, Biblical concepts. But there is a time and place for everything under Heaven (Ecclesiastes 3:1). Abusive situations are not the right time and place for putting yourself aside and turning the other cheek. For example, we would never say to a child abducted into sex trafficking "Oh, you need to put yourself aside— just turn the other cheek." Can you even imagine? Remaining in the torment of abusive darkness is oppression and captivity, not Godliness. But I didn't know that…I didn't know I was stuck in a stronghold of religious obligation built by the enemy, who was happy to quote scripture to me as I stayed there, small and broken. Never forget: the devil is the world's greatest manipulator (remember how he manipulated Eve in the garden?), and he knows the Bible better than you do.

I didn't know I was a captive. I lived a pretend life where I hoped and prayed that Kevin would soften toward me and the Lord. I pretended to be happy. Most people thought I was. I hoped at some point, Kevin would come around. But over the years, he didn't. In fact, the darkness surrounding him only increased. And all my pretending seemed to have reached its maximum capacity. That day at coffee with Claire, the pretense came to an end. And when she said to me that I couldn't kiss him because of the way he spoke to me, scales fell off my eyes and I could see things I didn't see before.

I knew I had reached a point of no return. A decade of pain was tired of being stuffed away, and there was no stopping it from coming out. I couldn't have stopped it even if I tried. The door to my repressed agony had been cracked open, and I was not going to be able to close the door and keep pretending. My pain was going to have its day. And it might not be pretty.

OPENING THE SAILS OF MY HEART

Later that same day, Kevin was working on a project in our house. He needed more of a certain kind of screw and I volunteered to go to the hardware store. I wanted to get out of there, to get some air, and to think about what happened with Claire earlier in the day.

Driving home from the store, I had a terrible feeling in the pit of my stomach. I was not sure what to do with what had happened earlier in the day, but I knew the part of me ignoring my pain was no longer asleep. It was like waking up from a nightmare but with the horrible realization that it wasn't a dream, but my actual life. I could feel terrible, painful things in my heart, when I hadn't felt anything at all for years. And it didn't feel like warm fuzzies. I was terrified.

Every once in a while, I think God turns on a song that you need in that exact moment. On that drive home from the hardware store, a song called "Sails" by Pat Barrett came on. I had never heard it before—I have no idea how it got on my playlist. The lyrics said, *"I let out the sails of my heart, here I am, here you are. Oh Lord, set me free."* In that moment, with that perfect song, I gave my heart permission to open up its sails. My heart, stuffed full of secret pain for nearly a decade, cried out for freedom. I will never forget the exact street and location I was on when I said these words to God like a groan from the deepest place in my soul. Tears streamed down my face. I prayed, "God, please help me."

When I got home from the hardware store, Kevin knew something had changed. In the unseen realm, the facade had been removed. The lie was gone, the veil pulled back. I was not asleep anymore.

He asked, "What's wrong?"

"I am not okay," I replied.

"Don't leave me," he said. This marked the one and only time, both before and after that moment that I ever heard him say something truly humble.

"I won't," I said.

That night, I stopped drinking cocktails. I didn't try or struggle to stop, I just knew I didn't need a nightly tranquilizer anymore. I knew I needed to feel everything from that point forward. Now that I was awake, I wasn't going to try to numb my pain or go back to sleep. I was going to do something about it.

Let me ask you the same question Claire asked me that day. Are *you* okay?

CHAPTER ONE: THE DAY I WOKE UP

Are you living with an entire hidden well of heart pain? Are you sitting in a Bible study, pretending to be fine, but on the inside you're actually sick, frail, thin, hooked up to life support, and about to drown? Are you trying to be a good Christian by performing, pretending, pleasing, conforming, complying, and denying yourself, when this could actually not be the life God planned for you, but the life the enemy planned for you?

When Jesus went to the temple in Nazareth and read the scroll of the book of Isaiah, he announced why he had come to Earth. He came to heal the brokenhearted, to proclaim freedom to the captives, and to liberate the oppressed (see Luke 4:18-19). He came to break every curse introduced through sin in the garden. To those who have ears to hear, to those who awaken, there is complete freedom to be found in Jesus. The price he paid was enough to rescue you from even the deepest, darkest prison and to heal you one hundred percent. He makes all things new. There is power in the name of Jesus to give you a completely new life, where your pain is so far from you, that even the memory of it has no sting. He is able to do it. Anything short of that is less than the price Jesus paid for your freedom.

If you open up the sails of your heart—if you call to him for help, he will take you by the hand, and lead you out. It will be hard, and at times you might look back, like the Israelites leaving Egypt, and think you had it better when you were a slave, because at least then you knew what to expect. But there is a promised land out there, and God designed you to live in it. Take his hand.

QUESTIONS FOR THE READER:

1. Why did Jesus come to earth, according to Luke 4:18-19?

2. When Jesus spoke about the "captives" and the "oppressed," who do you think he was talking about?

3. Are you living with hidden, stuffed-away heart pain, and pretending to be okay, because you don't think you have another choice? If so, when you close your eyes and picture Jesus, what do you think he thinks about this? What is his desire for you?

4. What does it mean to "open up the sails of your heart?" Why is this important?

READ THIS PRAYER OUT LOUD:

God, I open up the sails of my heart to you. I invite your Holy Spirit to come and to give me eyes to see the places where I am living in captivity. I ask that you would give me a revelation of the hidden pain in my heart. I ask that you show me where I am pretending and living in religious obligation. And I ask that you would come with your truth and show me that your plans for me are great, plans to prosper me, not to harm me, and to give me a future and a hope. I come into alignment with the reality that Jesus came to Earth and paid the full price for my freedom, and that he desires for me to be free from every snare, trap, and shackle of bondage. I declare over myself that I am God's treasure, his beloved, that I was made for a great purpose, and that I was not made to live in constant pain. I ask for grace to fully awaken from a season of being asleep, so I may become all God made me to be. Jesus, I ask that you would take me by the hand and lead me out of captivity. I know it will not be easy, but I believe you are with me, you are for me, and you will never leave me. I decide now, in the name of Jesus, to put all my trust in you, God. Emmanuel, thank you for drawing near.

Chapter Two

RETURNING TO THE GARDEN

The man and his wife felt no shame, unaware that they were both naked.

Genesis 2:25 (TPT)

NAKED AND UNASHAMED

I woke up in the middle of the night with a vivid image burned into my mind. The image was the beautiful silhouette of a completely naked woman.

God had been speaking to me in unexpected ways since the day I woke up. It was a lot at once. It was almost like when a cork pops off a bottle because of the pressure inside, and the sudden release makes it explode everywhere. I felt like years of stopped-up things God wanted to speak to me, but I was unable to hear, were all being released now that I had awakened. And after nearly ten years of captivity, despite the sudden awareness and agony of my wounded, bleeding heart, I was ecstatic to be back to the place I had been many years before: the place where I was connected to God's heart and could easily hear him. And this vivid image of a naked woman was not just some dream or my imagination. I knew God put it there.

At first, I was kind of embarrassed. I thought to myself, *why am I seeing naked pictures?* But it wasn't sexual or erotic in any way. It was simply beautiful. When I asked God what it was about, I heard his still, small voice say, "Return to the garden."

I've noticed something about when God speaks to me. It often doesn't make a lot of sense at first—it's not usually something super obvious or anything that has already been floating through my head. When he speaks to me, my initial response is usually something like, "Huh? What do you mean?" His thoughts are higher than our thoughts (Isaiah 55:8-9).

He said to return to the garden. And while I didn't have the complete picture, I had a strong sense of where this was going. He wanted me to return to how he originally made me: naked, unashamed, and in perfect unity with God and a perfect equal with Adam. He was inviting me back to my original design and position, before I was marred by the fall, by sin, and its consequences. He wanted me to look and see what he intended for me, what he still had for me, and what it looked like to return to the garden, because Jesus had paid to return me there. At the time, I had no idea how important and fundamental this revelation would become to me—how important it is for all of us.

God's original design and intention for women is so beautifully and simply laid out in Genesis 1:26-28 (NKJV):

> *Then God said, "Let us make man in our image, according to our likeness; let them have dominion over the fish of the sea, over the birds of the air, and over the cattle, over all the earth and over every creeping thing that creeps on the earth." So God created man in his own image; in the image of God he created him, male and female he created them. Then God blessed them, and God said to them, "Be fruitful and multiply; fill the earth and subdue it; have dominion over the fish of the sea, over the birds of the air, and over every living thing that moves on the earth."*

God is neither male nor female (instead, he is Spirit - John 4:24), but he made both men and women in his image, in his likeness. That means that while they are very different in many ways, both men and women equally reflect God's characteristics. God gave dominion and rulership of the Earth to both men and women. He told them to subdue the Earth. Not to point out the obvious here, but when we go back to this first chapter of the book of Genesis and understand how God set up gender roles, there was no built-in hierarchy, there wasn't a primary leader, there wasn't a more important or wise one, there was not one over and one under. No, those structures that have been following humanity since the garden did not come from God's design at all, but as a consequence of sin.

Now if you're getting hung up on some translations calling Eve a "helper" in Genesis 2:18 (NKJV), let me briefly address that. And the Lord God said, "It is not good that man should be alone; I will make him a helper comparable to him."

The word sometimes translated as "helper" in this verse is the Hebrew word *'ezer*. According to the book of Genesis in The Passion Translation

(TPT), this word is used to describe God himself (as the "Helper") in the Bible fourteen times, and often in the context of military-type help. For example, the word "Helper" in Psalm 54:4 ("Behold, God is my Helper") is *'ezer*. It could be accurately translated as "strong rescuer." Eve was made to be a strong rescuer to Adam, just like God, himself, can be our strong rescuer—not a subservient underling.

THE CURSE

Unfortunately, the perfection of God's original design for the unity and equality of men and women was short-lived. We know how the story goes in Genesis chapter three: the devil, in the form of a snake, convinced Eve to eat the fruit from the tree of the knowledge of good and evil. He succeeded in manipulating her, saying, "Did God really say?" Eve ate the forbidden fruit, gave some to Adam, and he also ate it. Immediately, they realized they were naked, and they were ashamed.

When God confronted them, they hid. Adam immediately blamed Eve, and Eve immediately blamed the devil. Let's be clear: both Eve and Adam sinned—it wasn't just Eve. And the consequences of sin were dire indeed: great hostility between the devil and the woman, the increased difficulty in childbirth for the woman, the requirement for man to toil and labor all his days, and ultimately, the curse that would set women in every generation down a disastrous path: "Your desire shall be for your husband, and he shall rule over you" (Genesis 3:16b, NKJV).

Sin separated humans from God, but this was not the only consequence. Sin also separated men and women. I believe that every single dysfunctional relational pattern between men and women in every generation in history can find its root in what happened in Genesis chapter three. There are a few important outcomes from this scripture: first, the pattern of the woman being weak-willed and manipulated by the devil; second, the pattern of the man blaming the woman when confronted with his choice to sin (this is the world's very first example of gaslighting - thanks, Adam); and third, the pattern of both men and women hiding in shame and separation from God as a reaction to sin. But the last and most disturbing outcome is the pattern that a woman's desire would be for her husband, and that he would rule over her. A man's rulership over a woman was a pattern born from the curse of sin.

None of these patterns were God's plan or design for us, and all of them were direct results of sin and the fall. They've also been repeating themselves since the very first man and woman. When we recognize them in the world, we must not justify them because they've been around so long, but we should see them for what they are: a curse! When we see belief systems that support the notion that it's the man's role to lead and the woman's role to submit, we can trace this back to original sin and the curse in Genesis three. Most people don't realize that these commonplace patterns of male superiority and rulership aren't God's design but a direct result of the curse. The problem isn't limited to misconception and lack of understanding—some Christian circles have actually adopted patterns from the curse as "gender rules" for their constituents, setting up standards for how men are to rule and women are to submit. Much of traditional Christian culture has actually memorialized the curse as "how we do things."

The consequences of the fall for women in history has been nothing short of catastrophic. That may sound dramatic, but if the design for men and women was in fact perfect equality and shared dominion, then <u>every</u> culture since the fall has missed the mark significantly. There has never been a culture or society where men and women were actually equals. Some generations and cultures have come closer to God's design than others, and Jesus himself could be considered the greatest proponent of women's equality who ever lived. But in modern day, even in the church, patterns of male hierarchical superiority are alive and well and still a mainstream pattern of thought.

Let me give you some examples. Almost every Christian I know is familiar with the text in Ephesians chapter five suggesting a woman "submit" to her husband, but significantly fewer Christians I know are equally familiar with the larger portion of Ephesians five that outlines a man's obligation toward his wife: to serve and care for her so fully, that it looks like Christ serving the church. We sometimes lack the bigger picture that Ephesians five presents a model of mutual submission between husbands and wives, not a model of male domination. Or as another example, most

CHAPTER TWO: RETURNING TO THE GARDEN

Christian women I know believe their husband is supposed to be the sole "spiritual leader" of their home. They've never been offered the possibility that God didn't intend for it to be that way. Women are to lead and share dominion at the same level of authority and rulership as men, according to Genesis chapter one. Assigning a man as the primary "spiritual leader" not only strips a woman from her place of shared God-given spiritual leadership, but creates a potential idolatry situation where a woman submits to her husband instead of to God, and obeys her spouse before her maker.

But there is great hope. Jesus is the answer to these problems. His response is not an angry feminist manifesto, because he is gentle and lowly (Matthew 11:29). He left his place at the right hand of the Father and came to Earth as a man to show us the right way to live, and to become the sacrifice that would pay the price for our sin once and for all time. Jesus has actually paid the full price to return us all to our original place in the garden: the place of full connection and intimacy with God, and the place of full connection and intimacy between men and women. The separation caused by sin is now abolished. The veil has been torn. The curse has been broken. We can return to our place, naked and unashamed in the garden, because of what Jesus has done. We can return to full intimacy with God and with each other! This is the gospel - the greatest news the world has ever received.

If that's true—and any Bible-believing person would have a really hard time arguing that it's not—then why haven't believers in Jesus returned to the garden? Why are most of us still living so distant from God (naked and ashamed), and why is there still so much brokenness between men and women?

We must not forget that the devil's primary goal is to keep us from stepping into what Jesus purchased and taking our positions of authority as kings and priests (Revelation 1:6). Jesus said that all those who follow him will do all the same things he did on Earth and even greater things (John 14:12). This includes healing the sick, casting out demons, and raising the dead. The enemy obviously doesn't want believers to move in that authority, and, unfortunately, he's been largely successful. How many Christians do you know who regularly heal the sick and raise the dead?

PRIDE AND RELIGION

In the context of the relationships between men and women, I believe the devil uses two primary tactics to keep us from the fullness of what the cross purchased: pride and religion. Both men and women are susceptible to both of these deceptions, but the enemy has been particularly successful in tactics of pride with men, and particularly successful in tactics of religion with women. Of course not every man has a problem with pride, nor does every woman have a problem with religion. And some men struggle with religion, and some women struggle with pride. But there are some big strategies of the enemy where he has been plundering humans for centuries, and they must be exposed so they may be addressed.

Pride has its root in envy and insecurity, and it has a hard time being humble, correctable, or teachable. In relationships, pride in men manifests as the need to exert power, authority, or rulership over others, especially women. It believes they are greater, and they have a need to be greater. They draw their strength from the woman being lesser. Pride manifests as behaving as strong and powerful, but it's a false strength because it's rooted in darkness, envy, manipulation, and sin. I believe many men gravitate toward belief systems that make them the "head" of the wife because this feeds the carnal, prideful flesh. Men operating in pride have a need to hold a position above their spouse. They feel the need to remind their wife of the requirement to look to him for decisions, and they become insecure when their spouse is elevated, celebrated, promoted, or otherwise operates in authority of any kind. If we are going to see any significant breakthrough in women returning to their original design, this issue of pride will need to be addressed. Men must also return to the garden and be restored to their original design. But that is perhaps the topic of another book (not this one!).

Religion, simply put, is pretending. It's outwardly going through the motions of being good and righteous, but inwardly, our hearts are disconnected. If the cross says, "you never have to pay your debt, because Jesus paid," then religion says, "you are not good enough, so you need to pay." Religion imposes rules that are criteria for acceptance. While God designed us for intimacy, religion tries to be accepted by God (and by men) through servanthood. Women are significantly more susceptive to this deception. In relationships, religious strongholds manifest in women as people-pleasing, conforming, complying, and staying small to avoid punishment. Religion in women masquerades as Godly humility, but is actually just trying to earn acceptance by performance and self-sacrifice. Religion is the greatest affront to the cross because it tries to earn acceptance when the price was already paid in full by Jesus. If we are going to see significant breakthrough in women returning to their original design, religious strongholds will need to be addressed.

But - Jesus. I think very few people alive today or who have ever lived have fully understood the magnitude of what Jesus purchased on that cross. When he said, "It is finished," he meant that the entire cost to return every child of God to their original place in the garden had been paid. The veil was completely torn, but the hard part is—we still have to walk through the torn veil to find the fullness of God on the other side. That involves our choices. Returning to the garden goes against every cultural norm that has been established following the curse, so it won't look or feel like what everyone else is doing. Finding complete freedom in Jesus is free, but it's not without great cost.

I know from my own experience that making the choice to leave captivity— to break agreement with religious strongholds and obligation, and step into the freedom offered by Jesus—can be the most terrifying choice a woman will ever make. Fear and religious duty are powerful opponents. But there is a whole new life on the other side. Adam and Eve always had choices in the garden, and we still have all our choices now. Let us be the generation of women that chooses to walk through that torn veil into new life.

QUESTIONS FOR THE READER:

1. What views do you have of the roles of men and women that might not be aligned to God's perfect design outlined in Genesis chapter one?

2. Do you think men and women could be equals, but still be very different? What parts of God's image do you think are uniquely reflected in women, and which parts are uniquely reflected in men?

3. Which patterns of the curse described in this chapter can you identify in your own life, in society, and in the church?

4. Do you see any places where the enemy's strategies of pride or religion are operating in your life?

5. Do you believe the price Jesus paid was enough to return you to the fullness of intimacy with God, and the fullness of intimacy in relationships? What are the things keeping you from stepping into that reality?

READ THIS PRAYER OUT LOUD:

God, thank you for your word and for revealing to me your original design for men and women. Thank you that Jesus paid the full price, not only to restore us to intimacy with you, but to restore the stolen intimacy and connection between men and women. Holy Spirit, I ask that you would search me and show any places in my heart, mind, and spirit where my beliefs do not align with your truth. I ask that you would give me a personal revelation of how you designed me and how you made me for connection with you and with others. I ask that you renew a right Spirit in me. Come,

Spirit of God, and lead me into the fullness of freedom that was purchased by Jesus through his death and resurrection. Remove any deception and gently correct me, because you are a loving father. I thank you for the grace to see clearly, even if it's different from what I thought before. Thank you for leading me into truth and freedom, in the name of Jesus.

Chapter Three

INTO CAPTIVITY

Be sober, be vigilant; because your adversary the devil walks about like a roaring lion, seeking whom he may devour.

1 Peter 5:8 (NKJV)

RELIGION IS EMPTY

Let me start at the beginning. I grew up without having a relationship with God. Don't get me wrong—I was a Christian who believed in Jesus, and I went to church multiple times a week. I tried to "be good," and I went to a Christian college. I didn't have premarital sex. But I never really met God. I never knew him as a person. I never knew he liked me, or that he even loved me. Sure, I heard all the "Jesus loves you" songs and statements, but it didn't register or penetrate my heart. My biggest priority as far as God was concerned was to mess up as little as possible so I could make it to Heaven and not be in trouble. I didn't actually have a personal experience with God until much later. Sadly, I think much of the body of Christ is in this boat. It's a powerless religious life and certainly not the one described in the New Testament.

I've thought a lot, across many years, about why this is the case. In the end I've come to this conclusion: experiential Christianity, where we encounter God as a person and as a friend, a God who speaks, who supernaturally moves, who is unpredictable but thrilling—is really scary for those who seek the comfort of control and a black and white formula for how to live right. In other words, experiential Christianity (which is how Jesus lived—and how the church operated in the book of Acts) pulls us out of our comfort zone of self-reliance and "good person" checklists into the realm of having to rely on manna from Heaven each day. It is more about relationships than regulations. And for many, that's just too messy.

I had always been afraid of not being good enough. In high school, I tried to be everything. I was accepted in the popular crowd, I made the varsity track team my freshman year, and I got a perfect 4.0 grade point average. But I was totally empty. Unconsciously, my greatest fear was that I would not be beautiful enough, athletic enough, or academic enough, and others would see my weakness. I was a track and field state champion, and I was class valedictorian. But I was also rebellious. I lied to my parents about where I was going out at night. I kissed a lot of boys, drank alcohol occasionally, and partied. On the surface I was well-liked, moderately good-looking, and successful. I went to youth group regularly and tried to read my Bible like I was supposed to. I once had a friend say to me, "How do you do it – you are good at everything you do and also beautiful - you have it totally made!" But at the end of my senior year, I felt like a total failure. I felt empty with all my friends. There was no depth to my life. I had no joy in anything. I was a complete fraud. And the worst part was that I still felt I was nowhere near good enough. It was just a matter of time until everyone realized what a mess I really was.

I made the choice toward the end of my high school senior year to attend an out-of-state Christian college. I needed to start over. I wasn't sure what was wrong, and I didn't stop to think that much about it. I stopped hanging out with my high school friends, I stopped returning their calls, and I started over in a new place with new people.

Christian college was where I met Henry. I had become friends with his sister, who was beautiful, confident, fashionable, and popular. Before I met him, Henry's sister would talk about how handsome, athletic, and amazing he was. She said she didn't believe any girl at our college would be good enough for him.

Back then I was not Spirit-filled, and all kinds of wrong emotions and unhealthy desires ruled my life unchecked. I operated in the spiritual reality of life after the fall: bound up in religious duty, disconnected from intimacy with God, and trying to perform to be good enough for God and for others. I was competitive and insecure. So I'm sure you know where this is headed. I decided in my heart that I was going to be the girl who won Henry—I would prove to his sister and everyone else that I was good enough. I wanted to be the girl that was best, the one he chose. And when I met him, I agreed that he was athletic, funny, and handsome.

CHAPTER THREE: INTO CAPTIVITY

EVERYWHERE BY FLEETWOOD MAC

One of my most vivid memories of dating Henry was when we drove out to the countryside with some friends to try to get away from the city lights and see a meteor shower. In the car on the way, the song "Everywhere" by Fleetwood Mac came on the radio. This was a childhood favorite of mine, so I did what any smitten girl would do in this situation—I proceeded to sing it to Henry. *"Ooooohh, I want to be with you everywhere."* I was just being myself and showing affection for him through music.

His reaction was complete disgust. "Stop singing," he said. "You're making me uncomfortable." Henry's friend was taken aback by this response, and said, "Man, I would do anything for a pretty girl to sing that song to me!" I think the friend was as perplexed about Henry's response as I was.

I've always loved to sing, and I grew up in a musical family. My parents were in a band, they sang in the church choir for three services on Sundays, and I learned to hear and sing harmonies just being in the car with them. I was the kind of kid that got teased for constantly singing at the dinner table. Songs were always coming out of me.

So that moment when Henry silenced me, something died inside. From this point forward, I felt like I wasn't supposed to sing in front of him, for risk of annoying him or making him uncomfortable. I was also not supposed to share feelings from my heart, like "wanting to be with him everywhere." There were unspoken rules forming in our relationship, and they all revolved around me behaving in a way that didn't elicit a negative response from him. My behavior was being shaped by his moods and reactions. I came into agreement with the lie that I needed to be small, compliant, and submissive so Henry wouldn't get upset and punish me.

In my family growing up, like most other families I knew, talking about feelings and emotions wasn't the norm, so not talking about feelings or emotions with Henry also felt "normal." Neither Henry nor I had any tools on how to navigate a healthy relationship, how to communicate effectively, or how to keep our hearts open to each other. And not opening my heart felt like a very safe way to live, especially when he routinely wounded me with his sarcasm and cutting criticism. I definitely did not want to feel vulnerable.

Operating in whatever way was required for me to manage Henry's moods and insecurities became my top priority. Our relationship was already headed for disaster.

NARCISSISTIC TENDENCIES

I graduated college summa cum laude with a triple major and a minor, after studying abroad for a year in Latin America. I returned home from college and got a great job right away at a global, Fortune 500 company. Henry and I were still together.

Everything was about proving I was good enough for him, and good enough to become part of his family. We went to his church, his family's Sunday dinners, and hung out with his friends. I was so focused on being good enough for him and trying to fit in with his family that I failed to see what was happening in the dynamic of our relationship. Not only did we have almost zero personal or emotional connection to one another, but Henry still didn't treat me particularly nice. His constant sarcasm was sharp, and it hurt. Jokes at my expense were common. We didn't talk about feelings or important issues, and our relationship was completely surface-level. And my connections with my own family and friends diminished quickly.

When Henry proposed, I said yes. I don't remember feeling anything except relief that I had finally gotten what I wanted. Wasn't it what I wanted? Since I had poured all my effort into Henry and his family, I didn't really have any close friends who could see below the surface and bring up the obvious issues. No one said anything to me like, "Are you sure about marrying him?" No one was close enough to see. And I projected all sorts of pretend emotions: contentment, joy, and security. How I really felt was afraid, unloved, and fearful of the future.

I set up an appointment for us with a pre-marriage counselor through one of my work benefits. The counselor was a tenured therapist with many years of couples counseling experience. During our appointment, he asked probing questions about our relationship, and I remember not being able to stop myself from crying. I remember the counselor asking Henry questions, and Henry becoming increasingly agitated. I remember the counselor saying something about Henry having narcissistic tendencies. I didn't know what that meant. I had never heard of "narcissistic tendencies." The counselor said we had a lot of work to do if we wanted to have a successful relationship.

Henry was mad in the car as he drove me home from counseling. He said the counselor was an idiot, and that he was not going back. But I wanted to go back. The counselor had uncovered some things I really identified with. Someone had seen my side and had come to my defense, and I didn't want to go back to it being hidden. Henry and I argued. Finally, he gave me a choice: if I wanted to marry him, we were done with this counselor. Instead, he wanted to meet a few times with the pastor of his family's church, and that would be enough.

That night at home in my parents' house, I cried harder than I ever had. I thought about how my dad treated me: kind, with affection, and with love. Henry didn't treat me that way, but I had a choice to make. It was basically to accept him "as-is," and hope that he would soften and change over time, or it would be over. And I would be alone. I would have failed at something I worked so hard for. I wept and wept, for what felt like hours.

And then I did something that would become the most destructive pattern of my life. I chose to stuff it all down, push it deep and far away, and to marry Henry anyway. That night, I decided the best plan was to "just go to sleep" and that I would feel better in the morning. It would all be fine. I was really deceived.

I don't live with regrets, but I do look back and see where I made mistakes. In this particular moment, when I chose to stuff my pain down and marry a man who was cruel to me, I gave the enemy full access to torment me. Just as the curse said, my desire would be for my husband, and he would rule over me.

A PASTOR WHO SAW NOTHING WRONG

Henry and I had several pre-marital counseling sessions with his senior pastor, who was going to conduct our wedding ceremony. Everyone at the church loved Henry, and he was seen as a bit of a golden child. He was the star of the church softball team and the church flag football league. He was the youngest of four children, and his three older sisters adored him. In the eyes of everyone who knew him, he could do no wrong.

The pastor took us through some standard workbook pages and prayed with us a few times. He never even got close to seeing or identifying the real dynamic of our relationship. He didn't ask how Henry treated me. He didn't review Ephesians chapter five which outlines how a healthy relationship has components of mutual submission, and discusses the role of a husband—to treat the wife with tender care and concern, as Jesus cares for the church. He didn't go anywhere below the surface. He didn't know Henry and I were not emotionally connected, or that my heart was already bruised and battered from a few years of sarcasm, cruelty, and lack of affection and kindness.

The pastor thought it was good to get married as soon as possible since we were waiting to have sex. He quoted 1 Corinthians 7:9, "It is better to marry than to burn with passion." Looking back, this was terrible marriage counseling. While it would be easy to blame the pastor in this situation, he was just doing what he knew to do. Much of the Christian ecosystem around marriage is deeply entrenched in centuries of dysfunction (that have become norms) resulting from the fall and the curse in the garden.

I thought if the pastor didn't see a problem, then maybe there was nothing wrong. I thought perhaps everyone's marriage started like this and true connection happened with time. Maybe love was only a choice, and I needed to just make the choice to love Henry unconditionally and forgive his shortcomings.

WOUNDED AND VULNERABLE

Henry and I got married in a small ceremony on a Monday in the mountains. It was cold outside. No one looked happy in our wedding pictures. Maybe everyone knew it was a mistake. Henry's parents were fighting on our wedding day so the lunch reception after the ceremony was full of awkward tension. I didn't feel joy or sadness—I felt nothing. I had checked out emotionally from our relationship a long time before that.

Six months into our marriage, not much had changed. I was still trying to please him and his family, and I grew more and more distant from my own family and friends. I tried hard to cook as well as his mother and his sisters. I went to their church and didn't feel anything. I joined the worship team, but I had become so insecure about singing, it was a painful experience. I felt I might never be good enough…always running to try to please and keep up with Henry and his perfect family. I exercised frequently, trying to be perfect for him. His response was to give me a warning, "You're becoming obsessed with working out." I couldn't win.

A man at work named Mauricio started chatting with me. At first it started with me practicing Spanish with him, making sure I didn't lose what I had learned while studying abroad in college.

But then he started asking me if my husband told me how beautiful I was. He asked me if my husband appreciated me. He asked if I was happy and loved. He asked if my husband danced with me. He pushed all the right buttons. I wasn't told I was beautiful. I wasn't appreciated, happy, or loved. Henry refused to dance with me. Henry and I had no connection and no intimacy. We never had.

Mauricio told me what my heart longed to hear. He told me I was worth more, that I was valuable, and that he loved me. He said he was a Christian, too. I was so desperate, starving for affection, that I let him in. I didn't have a physical relationship with Mauricio while I was married to Henry, but I had a very emotional affair with him. I believed he loved me. I was completely deceived.

THE DIVORCE

I confronted Henry by telling him I was tired of how he treated me, that I wasn't going to live my whole life with someone who didn't care for me. I rashly printed out divorce papers and asked him to sign.

Henry was shocked and surprised. After all, for our entire relationship I had been silent and compliant, not complaining about his treatment.

He denied any wrongdoing. He refused to entertain even the smallest possibility that he was part of the problem in our relationship. He took the divorce papers and went to stay with his parents for a few days. I expected him to come around and actually fight for me—to say he would do counseling and fix things. After all, we both grew up in a Christian setting where you just didn't divorce; divorce was for people who wanted to get tagged with a scarlet letter.

To my surprise, a few days later Henry stopped by to drop off divorce papers he had signed. He was apparently fine with it being over. He asked if there was someone else I was involved with. I said yes.

We had only been married for nine months so getting expensive attorneys didn't make sense. We scheduled an appointment with a court mediator to work out divorce specifics. Even though we had only been married for a short time, the mediator agreed with Henry that he was entitled to a significant portion of what I had accumulated in my savings and retirement accounts for the period of our marriage. Henry had a job, but I made a lot more money than he did. Henry even produced documents saying the townhouse we had purchased together (with my money) had appreciated in value during the few months of our marriage, and demanded I pay him in cash his portion of the equity if I wanted to keep it.

I didn't think it was fair that I was going to have to pay Henry—after all, he had a job and his own steady income—but I just wanted it to be over. I agreed to pay the full amount. We signed the papers, and just like that, my first marriage was over.

MAURICIO WAS A WARLOCK

I was now single and in a romantic whirlwind with Mauricio. After not having sex until I married Henry, I threw that all out the window now that I felt like Mauricio loved me and had shown me that I was worth being loved. He was completely different from Henry—he was thoughtful, danced with me, and made me feel amazing. He thought I was beautiful. It was nothing like being with Henry, who was indifferent towards my body and didn't connect with me emotionally at all.

CHAPTER THREE: INTO CAPTIVITY

Mauricio bought me an expensive watch and sunglasses. He seemed to like spoiling me. But he was married, and it appeared he would stay that way. He would go out late drinking with buddies from work and forget to call me or pick me up. He would be on the phone with me late at night and pass out during our conversations from drinking too much alcohol. The romantic high was wearing off, and I realized something wasn't right.

Perhaps the most disturbing part about Mauricio was when I realized he could see and watch me in my home when he wasn't there. He would get jealous of me spending time with others and would call later to say he had seen what I had been doing. I was no expert on the occult, but knew that spying on people through objects was called astral projection, and it was commonly used by Satan's followers—witches and warlocks—to manipulate and control others.

I am not sure what the final straw was that shook me back to reality, but I decided Mauricio was bad news. I told him not to call me or contact me in any way, and I decided it was time for me to go to counseling. I knew I was messed up. I had really believed he loved me. But he was no better than Henry, maybe even worse.

This was the lowest point of my life until that moment. In all the Christian circles I grew up in, only the biggest sinners and failures got divorced. In the denomination I grew up in, divorced people were not allowed to have ministry positions or be missionaries. And beyond the divorce, I had been lured into a sexual relationship with a follower of Satan. I was twenty-four years old, and I had screwed up my entire life. It was inexcusable.

DONNA THE COUNSELOR

My mom and dad knew a Christian counselor named Donna who had helped them through some hard seasons. They gave me her number, and I made an appointment right away.

In my first appointment with Donna, I could tell there was something really good and different about her. I didn't have this language then, but it was like the presence of God was in her office. It felt so peaceful to be there. It was safe and non-judgmental. Even though she was a Christian, there was no condemnation in her eyes toward me. I could let my defenses down and be honest. I told her about Henry and how ashamed I was for getting divorced, because I knew the Bible says God hates divorce. I told her about Mauricio and how ashamed I was of my sexual sin with him. I told her I felt like I was being crushed by the weight of my mistakes.

"First things first," Donna said. "You have a spirit of lust. You need to give Mauricio's witchcraft objects back to him and fully close that door. Then you need to tell the spirit of lust to leave. After that, we can work together to figure out how you got here, work on addressing the root causes, and focus on the Lord healing your heart."

Apparently, this was not your everyday Christian counseling. Please remember I was not a Spirit-filled Christian at this point—so not even remotely familiar with "spirits" and what it meant to tell them to leave. The most I knew about demonic spirits was probably something I had seen in a scary movie. Even though it was really shocking and not what I expected to hear from a counselor, I knew deep down what Donna said was true. I had been swept away and overtaken by lust and used by an evil man, who had been manipulating and controlling me. I needed to close the door to the darkness I had let in and get free.

For a moment while writing this, I wrestled with whether to include the details of the supernatural, active role of God in my story. I don't want to "turn off" readers who have never experienced God in such a personal way or make anyone uncomfortable who doesn't have the same views of the Holy Spirit as I do. But here is the unavoidable truth: the supernatural intervention of God himself and the power of the Holy Spirit was the only way I was able to overcome the darkness that had infiltrated my life. Nothing less would have been sufficient to achieve my freedom. Where the Spirit of the Lord is, there is liberty (2 Corinthians 3:17). His very nature is personal, and powerful enough to free any prisoner. So, I'm not going to keep the details from you. My story is full of impossible, powerful, intimate, and timely interventions of the supernatural power of God that all worked together to bring me out of the wilderness.

CHAPTER THREE: INTO CAPTIVITY

CLOSING THE DOOR

I packed up Mauricio's expensive gifts (a.k.a., his astral projection objects) in a bag and took them to work so I could return them and "close the door." I was afraid, because he was into some dark and powerful stuff. I knew this was not going to be easy.

By this time, I had been promoted and had my own office, so I went in, closed my blinds, and shut the door to get mentally prepared to return the gifts. I don't necessarily recommend randomly grabbing your Bible and asking God to point you to a verse—but I was so desperate for his help at this moment that I pulled out a small Bible from my bookshelf and asked God to help me. It was definitely the most sincere, most desperate, most faith-filled prayer I had ever prayed up until that point in my life.

God did not disappoint me. I opened directly to this passage in 2 Timothy 3:1-7 (NKJV):

> *"But know this, that in the last days perilous times will come: for men will be lovers of themselves, lovers of money, boasters, proud, blasphemers, disobedient to parents, unthankful, unholy, unloving, unforgiving, slanderers, without self-control, brutal, despisers of good, traitors, headstrong, haughty, lovers of pleasure rather than lovers of God, having a form of godliness but denying its power. And from such people turn away! For of this sort are those who creep into households and make captives of gullible women loaded down with sins, led away by various lusts, always learning and never able to come to the knowledge of the truth."*

I was completely floored. Mauricio might be the evil man described in this passage who crept into my household, but I was the gullible woman who had been led away by lust and sin.

This scripture was exactly what I needed to give me the confidence to do what needed done. I was finished being manipulated by an evil man, letting him into my house and my bed, and being led away by deception and lust. I wasn't scared anymore, I was mad. I was not going to be that gullible woman any longer.

I grabbed Mauricio's gifts and took the elevator to the floor where his office was. I knocked on his door and opened it. He seemed surprised to see me there. I wasted no time in placing the bag of gifts on his desk.

"I am closing the door," I said.

"Hold on!" he said. "Please let's talk about this. Please keep those gifts. Don't walk away."

"I don't want these gifts, and I'm closing the door, forever," I said, very firmly. And I closed his door and walked away. He didn't follow me.

I didn't know anything about deliverance and had received no training on expelling demonic spirits, but I knew I wanted this darkness gone. On the way back to my office, I told the spirit of lust that I had allowed into my life to leave. Walking down the hallway, I immediately started dry heaving. I had to stop at the restroom because I feared I was going to vomit. If I had eaten anything that morning, I probably would have. But I knew the spirit of lust was gone, because I had commanded it to go. The demonic only has access where we've given it permission, so revoking its access is how we get free. I knew Mauricio was behind me, too, and that I would never speak to him again. The door was closed.

More importantly, something new had started in me. I had felt God's presence in Donna's office. God had given me a specific scripture to give me the strength to break things off with Mauricio. I had used my authority to tell a spirit of lust that it must leave. After an entire life of dead works-based religion, I had a feeling something big was changing in my life. What if true Christianity was about more than trying to be good, following rules, and pleasing others? What if there was so much more?

QUESTIONS FOR THE READER:

1. Looking back on your life, are there moments you can identify when you decided to become small, compliant, or silent to manage the demands, moods, or insecurity of someone else?

2. Have you had significant moments when you decided to stuff your pain away and "just go to sleep?"

3. Do you know someone close to you who operates in any of the narcissistic tendencies of Second Timothy chapter three such as control, manipulation, and pride, or who have a form of godliness, but deny its power?

4. Are there areas of deception, like lust, where you need to close the door to the enemy and revoke the access he's had in your life?

READ THIS PRAYER OUT LOUD:

Holy Spirit, I invite your kind, searching gaze into my heart. I ask that you would highlight to me areas where I'm operating in a spirit of religious obligation, living in the fear of never being good enough. I ask that you would bring to light relationships and situations where my priority is remaining small, silent, obedient, compliant, and to conform to the demands and expectations of someone else. I repent now of serving someone else and centering my life and activities around the idol of another person. Holy Spirit, I ask that you renew a right Spirit within me. I ask that you would show me moments where I made a choice to stuff my pain away. Because of the price Jesus paid for me, I ask that you would take my hand and walk me out the places of bondage and captivity I've been living in and that you would let the light into the places of hidden pain in my heart, so I can begin to be healed. God, I restore you to your rightful place in my life, and I declare that I will no longer bow to the needs and expectations of others in a spirit of religious obligation, but I will serve you alone. I thank you that your plans for me are great, plans to prosper me, not to harm me, and to give me a future and a hope. I agree that your plan for me is to be liberated from any form of control, manipulation, and deception. Thank you, Jesus, that you came to Earth and paid the full price to free the captives, and to free me. And I declare that because Jesus overcame, that I too will overcome.

Chapter Four

GREAT AWAKENING

Then He who sat on the throne said, "Behold, I make all things new."

Revelation 21:5 (NKJV)

A DIFFERENT KIND OF CHURCH

My parents had been attending a charismatic church for a few years, and I had gone once or twice. This place was totally different from the church I grew up in. The few times I had been there, I thought it was weird. The worship portion of the service was long—like an hour—and the rest of the service was another hour. I wasn't super comfortable. I was used to a forty-five-minute church service where nothing particularly spiritual or deep happened.

But here I was, recently divorced from a cruel man, and recently broken up with a warlock who manipulated and controlled me. Even though I had broken free from these men, I felt like a complete and total failure.

I had felt God's presence in the counselor's office. I had heard God speak to me through the Bible the day I closed the door to Mauricio. I had actually expelled a demon of lust from myself. I was desperate to find hope and peace. So I started going regularly with my parents to their kind-of-weird church.

The first month of attending, I cried nonstop the entire worship service. I could not have stopped the tears even if I tried. People sang like God was actually listening. They waved flags, they danced, they kneeled…they didn't care what anyone else thought. And while the religious part of me was really offended, another part of me thought this was so beautiful and authentic. I saw people open their hearts to God and cry out to him as if he was near. I felt God's presence come into the room to meet his people. And while I had never seen this kind of intimacy in a church environment before, I slowly started to let God into my heart to transform it. I started to open my own mouth and sing. I started reading my Bible out of my own desire and hunger for his truth, and I believed he was going to speak to me. I realized from reading the book of Acts that believers in Jesus were never meant to live powerless lives, but to be filled with the Holy Spirit and power to overcome. I started to understand that God wasn't mad at me, that "He makes all things new," and freedom in Christ could be a reality in my life (see Revelation 21:5).

One Sunday the pastor talked about the importance of repentance. It wasn't a "you better repent or you're going to hell" kind of message, but more about how repentance leads us to freedom and breaking our chains of bondage to the past. I felt like the entire message was for me.

That day I went home after church and wrote some letters. I wrote a letter to Henry's sisters apologizing to them. I wrote one to his mom and dad saying sorry. Then I wrote one to Henry apologizing for having an emotional affair and asked him if we could meet.

Henry met me for coffee. He let me apologize to him for my emotional affair with Mauricio. He asked if we were still together, and I said no. I wasn't looking for an apology from Henry for the bad ways he treated me, nor did I get one. I was so focused on my wrongdoing, that I didn't think to point out to him that how he treated me was deeply wrong. But I felt like I had done the right thing in repenting for the wrong I had done toward the end of our relationship. It was good closure. We never spoke again after that.

Apologizing to Henry and his family had been hard, because I was ashamed. But it also didn't bring me the relief I had hoped it would. I was still covered in the constant, heaviness of shame. At this point, I still couldn't see the bigger picture here: the fact that I had pursued, dated, and married an extremely cruel man who trampled on my heart, and then gotten tangled up with a manipulator who had wormed his way into my home. I wasn't really aware that a pattern was repeating itself in my life, a pattern born out of the curse in the garden, one that would not stop repeating until I woke up and addressed it.

MY GREAT AWAKENING

My parents asked me if I wanted to attend a four-day conference focused on supernatural healing. Apparently a really well-known healing evangelist was coming to lead the event. It was all about the Biblical basis of supernatural healing and how to pray for the sick.

I think I really surprised my parents when I said yes. I didn't know what to expect, but I knew I was headed in the right direction. I had lived most of my life never actually believing that God could be actively involved in our lives. I had spent most of my life really far from his presence, power, and voice. Based on the little I had recently tasted, I knew there was more—that we were made for more. And I knew his active role in my life was the only thing keeping me from sinking into a pit of despair, guilt, and grief.

The teaching at this conference was straight out of scripture. The entire New Testament is built on the foundation that Jesus intended his followers to do all the things he did, and more. He said, "And these miracle signs will accompany those who believe: they will drive out demons in the power of my name. They will speak in tongues. They will be supernaturally protected from snakes and from drinking anything poisonous. And they will lay hands on the sick and heal them" (Mark 16:17-18, TPT).

It was incredible how many people were actually physically healed during this conference. I recall there being a word of knowledge (see 1 Corinthians 12:8) that God wanted to heal fibromyalgia, and after we all prayed, a whole line of women came up front to testify that all their pain was gone! Humans are made for supernatural things, and when we connect with that part of God, it is one of the most exciting things we can experience. It feels like returning to the garden, to the place where we walk with God in closeness and connection.

One lady I knew from church, who happened to be sitting by me during the first day, was jumping up and down because during the worship service, God had replaced her old dental fillings with gold. She let me see. I had no idea why God would do something so extravagant, but I knew this was a miracle, and I was excited for her. In fact, she felt outrageously loved and seen by God, and how could that ever be a bad thing? I had high expectations that this weekend was going to change my life. I had put God in a box, but he was about to blow my mind.

The first night of the conference, during the worship, I heard the most beautiful sound of a choir coming from the ceiling. At first I thought it was the sound of the worship team echoing around the sanctuary, but their mouths weren't moving when I heard this choir singing. Could this be angels? When the music ended, I found my dad and told him I thought I might have heard angels singing during worship. His reply was the best: "Yes! You heard them, too!?"

Nothing could have prepared me for what happened next. I'm not sure what the teaching was about that night. The message was probably great, but I can't recall it. All I remember is what happened at the end of the service during ministry time.

The person who spoke and ministered that night—a well-known itinerant healing evangelist, who had no idea who I was nor what I'd done and been through—pointed straight at me and gave me my first-ever prophecy. He said something like this:

"I want you to know that I've been divorced, too."

At this point, I was already sobbing.

"And I want to remind you what happened in Psalm 51 after David sinned with Bathsheba. He repented. God does not want sacrifices or works to make up for our mistakes, but only a contrite, repentant heart. God will <u>never</u> despise a humble heart.

And I can see that you are filled with regret and you don't feel you deserve to be forgiven. But you are humble and contrite and God gives grace to the humble. He forgives you. You can leave it behind you. Don't take it with you."

I was completely undone. How could this man know these things about me, unless God told him? The sheer supernatural power of this moment was the greatest thing I had ever experienced. But even greater was the message God was giving me: that he saw my repentant heart and just like he forgave and restored David for adultery (and murder), he forgave and restored me. I could leave it behind and stop it from haunting me my whole life. I didn't have to work to earn his forgiveness. My humbled, repentant heart was enough to make me clean.

I wish I could say that I got fully and completely set free from religion that night, but it ran pretty deep. The belief that I needed to work to please God, to make up for my mistakes, and to earn his love was still there, but it was like the sharp edge had been taken off. Sometimes freedom from long-term mindsets that stem from the fall and the curse aren't instantaneously reversed, but need time and a process to ultimately shift and align with God's word and design. I had started the process, but I still had a long way to go.

NEW SUPERNATURAL LIFE

I was new to all this—signs and wonders, supernatural healings, gold fillings, angels singing, and prophesy. I was starting to really see that God isn't some distant, angry monarch far away in Heaven, but a kind, present, personal friend who wants nothing more than to return us to the garden, to free us and to be connected with us. I had thought, like so many others do, that Jesus died just to get us to Heaven someday but in the meantime, we have to trudge through a painful life until we reach him on the other side. Not so! The freeing power of Jesus was for right now. I was so grateful he was rescuing me from my old life of dead religion.

I started attending the young adults group at church. I learned how to pray by listening to God. I received the infilling of the Holy Spirit (see Acts 1:8) and a prayer language (see Jude 1:20). I took several classes on the Biblical basis of prophecy and learned how to partner with God to prophesy to strengthen, encourage, and comfort others (1 Corinthians 14:3). I joined prophetic teams and heard and communicated God's heart for his people. I experienced God in my body, and once I felt him physically writing his name on my forehead (see Revelation 22:4). I wanted to find and experience every single thing that Jesus died to pay for. I realized we were never made to live each day without his supernatural power.

One of the best parts of this new season was how different it was when I read my Bible. It was like I was reading it for the first time with new eyes. I wondered how I had missed it all those years—how I had glazed over major Biblical themes about how Jesus intended for us to live how he lived, ministering to others with power that can shake the world out of despair, fear, and doubt. The same Spirit that raised Christ from the dead now lived in me (Romans 8:11)! Jesus said, those who believe in him will not only do the same works he did, but even greater works (John 14:12)!

Every person is made with a hunger and desire for the supernatural. God made us that way, because he is supernatural, and we are made in his image. The more I discovered about him, the more I knew I was still only scratching the surface. I had entered the grandest adventure imaginable where I was connected to the God of the universe and I could be part of what he was doing on Earth. I had never been so alive. This was my "great awakening." God wasn't dead, and neither was I! The Bible is full of men and women who made epic mistakes and God used them anyway. If they weren't disqualified, I wasn't either. Everything was possible, because he makes all things new, and he wasn't mad at me. He actually loved me, more than I could ever fathom.

MADRID

My church planned a ministry trip to Tanzania, and I decided to go. I had heard from so many people that one of the best ways to accelerate learning the ways of the Holy Spirit and to raise my faith in miracles was to go on a ministry trip to somewhere like Africa where supernatural healing, demonic deliverance, and signs and wonders were the norm.

I was able to plan the ministry trip around some work travel I had to do. My plan was to go to Madrid to speak at a conference I was invited to, then join the church team in Tanzania, and afterward, to continue on to some work meetings in Ghana. International travel for work had become pretty routine for me, and I was happy to do it. I especially loved the time I would spend with the Lord on long flights—journaling, listening to worship music, and reading books about healing evangelists like William Branham, Aimee Semple McPherson, and Kathryn Khulman.

I arrived in Madrid and checked into my hotel. The following day I was scheduled as a speaker at an industry conference. My company was doing really exciting, innovative things, and I was leading a big portion of it. And since someone at church had prayed for me and I had received freedom from the fear of public singing, public speaking had also become a lot more comfortable for me. I was really starting to enjoy it. After having been so painfully silenced by Henry, I was finding my voice again.

CHAPTER FOUR: GREAT AWAKENING

That night, I was up most of the night with supernatural dreams and visions. This kind of thing had never happened to me before. I dreamed that someone who would be at my conference the next day had a daughter who was sick with cancer. I dreamed that someone who would be there was struggling with depression. I dreamed that someone who would attend needed healing in their back.

In the morning, I was really conflicted about what to do. The very obvious reality was that God had revealed to me that he wanted to heal some people in my meeting. He was giving me an opportunity to minister. The other very obvious reality was that it didn't seem appropriate to call out words of knowledge for healing in a professional setting. Would I offend someone? This was a tricky situation, I was jet lagged, and I hadn't really slept at all.

I gave my presentation to a crowd of about a hundred people, and it was well-received. Then they quickly went on to the next speaker and presentation, before I could really say anything further. I stood in the back, feeling like I still needed to do something about my dreams the night before. I had to be brave. I had to trust the Lord. I remembered a prophetic word one of our pastors had recently given me that I was going to "blur the lines" between work and ministry. He said, "They are not separate, you must blur the lines." I felt like this was the moment to do it.

As the conference organizer stood to thank everyone for their participation and to dismiss, I felt myself quickly walking forward and asking for a few moments with the microphone. It was terrifying but I was doing it. The man had a confused look on his face, but he obliged.

I said, "Last night God spoke to me about some people in here. Someone has a daughter suffering from cancer, someone is dealing with depression, someone has pain in their back. If you want prayer, I will be up here, please come see me." And I gave the microphone back.

This was one of the bravest things I have ever done. I still can't believe I did it. And I stood there for a few minutes thinking no one was coming, but then a line started to form. I prayed for several people, then an older man approached with his female assistant. He introduced himself as the CEO of a very large mobile telecom company in the Middle East. He wanted me to pray for his assistant who was there with him because she had pain in her back and neck.

I prayed for his assistant and her pain left completely. Praise God! The CEO was amazed and excited. He asked if I would pray for him, too. I don't remember what I prayed, but I do remember the presence of the Holy Spirit coming into the room so powerfully during that prayer that it felt like the whole room was spinning.

When I finished praying, the CEO laughed and said to me, "Wow, it's the strangest feeling I have—I think I'm in love with you! Because I feel this overwhelming, powerful love that I have never felt before."

This was a perfect setup. "What you feel is the love of Jesus," I said. "He loves you so much and he wants you to know it. He is the way, the truth, and the life."

It's a moment I will never forget. God wanted this man to meet Jesus and experience his love. It was worth taking any career or personal risk.

I didn't keep in touch with the CEO or his assistant, and I didn't feel like I was supposed to. But I know my obedience in that moment was not insignificant— it created the potential for a Middle Eastern nation to be influenced by the love of Jesus received by one of their most powerful business leaders.

AFRICA

I met the team from church in Nairobi so we could connect to our final destination in Tanzania. I was full of faith, expectation, and enthusiasm about what God was going to do next. We were scheduled to hold several large services and to minister in many different regions.

What everyone said about going to Africa to minister was true. It is full of people who all believe in the supernatural realm. They believe in angels, demons, and the unseen powers of evil and good. Everywhere we ministered, nearly everyone was healed. I'm not exaggerating—several blind and deaf were healed, a man with a broken leg was completely healed and threw his crutches away. As I prayed for sweet person after person, I kept hearing this scripture from Galatians 5:1: "It is for freedom that Christ has set us free."

In the bus on the way to minister to a church full of widows who were gathered, something happened to me that had never happened before. I had been routinely speaking at work conferences and events, and I was starting to feel like public speaking was going to be an important part of my life. But I had never spoken in a church setting, and I lacked the confidence for preaching. I had plenty of confidence in business speaking, but not so much on the spiritual side. In the bus, God began to tell me what to say in the meeting with the widows. It was like a "knowing"—I knew exactly what words needed to be said. I heard them in my Spirit and I organized them in my mind.

When we got there, the team leader asked if anyone was feeling something from the Lord and wanted to speak. I raised my hand right away. I didn't have to muster something up, God had already given me exactly what to say.

God's message to these widows was about rising above our circumstances, rising up with wings like eagles, to see things from Heaven's perspective. We all have problems, a past, and pain filled with real issues. God doesn't necessarily always take away the hard circumstances, but he wants to change our perspective. He wants us to see with eternal eyes. He wants us to "come up higher" and see how he sees. And from his angle, our problems seem so much smaller. He gives us eyes to see what he sees, and this changes everything. It is far greater to ask for a new perspective than to ask for new circumstances.

In that moment I knew I was called not only to speak in business settings, but in spiritual settings, too. I was so excited about everything that was happening, and I fully surrendered to him and his purposes for me on Earth. I could not imagine a greater life than this life—alive with the Holy Spirit.

Despite all the freedom I had received and how near to the Lord that I felt, one important factor remained: I hadn't yet had the time with Donna the counselor to really work through all the root causes of how I ended up in a serious relationship with not one, but two manipulative, narcissistic men. Yes, I was filled with the Holy Spirit, but that didn't necessarily solve the underlying patterns of brokenness that had marked my life. Dysfunctional patterns that aren't fully addressed are always doomed to repeat themselves.

QUESTIONS FOR THE READER:

1. Are you living with places of guilt and shame, where God sees your repentant heart, and like David in Psalm 51 (and me at the healing school), God wants to remove your regret and mistakes and give you permission to leave them behind you?

2. After reading the book of Acts, how does your life line up (or not) with the Spirit-filled church that Jesus left on Earth?

3. Why do you think so many believers in Jesus are not operating in the signs, wonders, and miracles that Jesus said would follow those who believe in him according to Mark 16:17-18? What can/should be done about this?

4. Have you ever experienced the infilling of the Holy Spirit promised in the book of Acts, with the evidence of speaking in tongues? If Jesus said "you will receive power" when the Holy Spirit comes upon you, what does it look like to be a believer in Jesus without the Holy Spirit coming upon you?

5. If Jesus came to set the captives free, and He left us with the Holy Spirit, what do you think is the role of the Holy Spirit in Jesus setting the captives free today?

6. Can you observe any underlying dysfunctional patterns that repeat in your life, such as ending up with cruel or abusive men?

READ THIS PRAYER OUT LOUD:

Jesus, I believe your word, and I believe that you said those who follow you would do the same things you would do on Earth: heal the sick, raise the dead, and cast out demons. I thank you that you sent the Holy Spirit, so we can receive power, walk with you daily, and do even greater works than you did on Earth. Holy Spirit, I believe you are the Spirit of God that Jesus sent us when he left Earth. I believe that I will receive power— the same power that raised Jesus from the dead—as you fill me up. I invite you now to come upon me, to displace all darkness in me, to overwhelm me with your goodness, and to give me a supernatural prayer language. Thank you that it's not by might, or by power, but through your Spirit. Jesus, apart from you, I can do nothing. Thank you for being present, for being with me, and for filling me up according to your word. Thank you that you haven't called me a servant, but a friend. Teach me how to walk with you, to abide in your presence, to abide in the vine, and to begin a journey of living in the supernatural power you purchased for me on the cross. Everything is possible in you.

Chapter Five

BACK INTO BONDAGE

Let me be clear, the Anointed One has set us free - not partially, but completely and wonderfully free! We must always cherish this truth and stubbornly refuse to go back into the bondage of our past.

Galatians 5:1 (TPT)

KEVIN

It was the last night of my church ministry trip to Tanzania, and I was sitting and talking with two friends, Rachel and Kevin. I had asked them to pray for me, that I would have a safe and successful next leg of my trip to Ghana, where I was headed for work meetings, as the church team was headed home the next day.

We got to talking about my job and my boss, and the topic of my "husband list" came up. My boss, who was like a father-type figure to me, had told me that he and his wife had both made a list of everything they wanted in a spouse before they met, and it made it a lot easier to find the right person because they were both really clear on the kind of person they wanted. He encouraged me to write my own husband list, so I took the time to sit down and write out specific things that were important to me. I definitely wanted to get married again, to a really different kind of person than Henry had been. And I was really different now, too—I thought I knew a lot better what I wanted.

Kevin, Rachel, and I spent a lot of time ministering together during the trip, so when the two of them asked me to share my husband list, I was happy to do it. I opened my journal and read the list out loud.

What happened next seemed to come out of nowhere.

Kevin said, "Your list completely describes me."

I was shocked and kind of uncomfortable. I immediately said, "Well, I must be missing something from my list, because it's not you, Kevin."

We laughed it off but something had shifted with Kevin. He wasn't joking.

After my business in Ghana, I was in the Accra airport waiting to board my flight home, when I got an email from Kevin. He wanted to hang out when I got home. I didn't think Kevin was the husband that I was waiting for, but I was flattered that he was interested. I agreed to hang out.

Kevin became sure very quickly that I was the woman that he was supposed to marry. He said his mother "knew" his wife would be a friend first. And Kevin and I had shared some really deep spiritual experiences together in Africa. He went to my Spirit-filled church and seemed to be on the same page as far as God was concerned.

We started hanging out frequently, then we started dating. And we began to be together all the time, every day. It seemed like a lot kind of quickly, but he was so sure this was God's plan. He said God told him he would marry me. And the fact that he was so sure made me feel good about it. Kevin seemed to not hold my past against me, when one of my greatest fears was still that I would be judged for my past mistakes. Maybe this was the right man for me?

PEOPLE PLEASER

I was still seeing Donna the counselor on a regular basis. We had worked through the Mauricio stuff. We had spent time working on helping me see myself how God sees me, and accepting and forgiving myself.

Donna gave me a long list of "Who I Am in Christ" statements with scriptures to back up each. It was slow going, trying to actually believe what God thought about me, but I was working on it. Most importantly, she was helping me figure out why I made the choice to marry Henry in the first place. She was helping me unpack my religious fear (with corresponding recurring nightmares) that God wanted me to re-marry Henry because divorce was wrong. Donna was helping me see that God didn't want me to return to a marriage where I was being mistreated, because that's not his nature. She said his will for me was never to be mistreated by others, especially a spouse. But the spirit of religious obligation still had a hold on me.

One of our goals in counseling was to get to the root of what happened with Henry to make sure history didn't repeat itself. Why had I chosen and married a man who treated me poorly, a man who withheld kindness

CHAPTER FIVE: BACK INTO BONDAGE

and picked on me, a man I couldn't be myself with? Donna gave me a book to read about "people pleasers." She obviously thought this was where I needed to focus in order to become healthy.

On a flight headed to meet Kevin, my mom, and a few of our church leaders at a supernatural conference in Pennsylvania, I read most of Donna's people pleaser book. Seldom had I ever been so sick to my stomach. This book was clearly about me! It defined a people pleaser as someone who doesn't have healthy personal boundaries, and someone who habitually does what others want, only to wake up later and realize they've lost themselves and actually enabled the dysfunctional behavior of others. Reading it, I couldn't stop crying. I was filled with self-loathing. How could I have had this people-pleasing problem my whole life, and I was only now finding out about it?

This book explained so much. It explained why I had a lifelong pattern of unhealthy friendships where I never needed anything and it was all about the other person, only to burn out and abruptly disconnect from them in the end. It explained why I married Henry, only to wake up nine months later to realize I was completely alone, and the person I had been working so hard to please didn't even see me, except to tell me when he didn't like my hair, my weight, my clothes, or my cooking.

The worst part about this epiphany is that it made me partially responsible for what had happened with Henry: my people-pleasing tendencies and lack of boundaries had led me to marry someone cruel and indifferent. He was responsible for his own bad behavior, but I was responsible for my own choices—choices of staying small, silent, and compliant so I could save myself the pain of being rejected or the wounded pride of not being the girl that was good enough for him.

Another really troubling part of this epiphany was that it highlighted some big red flags in my relationship with Kevin. Now that I had some basic education on people pleasers, I suddenly became concerned that I might be people-pleasing him. Was I with him because it was what he wanted and I didn't want to disappoint him? Was I with him because some people at our church thought we made a great couple and I didn't want to disappoint them? Was I in touch at all with what I wanted?

There were some other concerning things, too. Kevin said he missed me constantly and wanted to be with me every night of the week with no breaks. I didn't want to say that I needed space because I didn't want to hurt his feelings. He also seemed to get strangely jealous when I prayed for other people or when we were in a group and the discussion focused on me and not him.

I could not stop crying as I exited the plane and on the drive to the conference as these realities hit me. I was confused and disoriented, like a rug had been swept out from under me. When I arrived at the conference, I was still reeling. Kevin asked me what was wrong, and I told him the book from my counselor upset me and that I really needed some space. He became agitated. Was I trying to break up with him, he asked? Why was I pushing him away? Why was I doing this to him out of nowhere? It wasn't fair to him, he said. I should calm down and stop being so emotional. It was all about him.

Being the people pleaser that I recently discovered I was, this reaction devastated me. I didn't want to upset him. Not pleasing him was the worst thing I could think of, because it made me feel rejected, like I was not good enough.

THE IDOL OF INDEPENDENCE

My emotions were churning, and I needed help. I asked a woman named Sandra, who was at the conference, for counsel. Sandra worked for the ministry hosting the conference and was quite a bit older than me, so she seemed like a safe person to confide in. I spilled my heart about counseling with Donna and the people pleaser book, how it made me feel, and how I didn't want to be a people pleaser. I told her all my instincts were telling me to end it with Kevin. I thought I was people-pleasing him, and I didn't want to be that kind of person. I didn't want to enable the bad behavior of others. I wanted to end the vicious cycle that had been repeating itself in my life: someone wanted me, so I gave them all of me, without regard to what I wanted or needed….only to find out I had given too much, and I wanted to escape.

CHAPTER FIVE: BACK INTO BONDAGE

I am convinced that what happened next was one of the cleverest strategies the devil has ever used against me. It would send me into a decade-long exile into darkness and captivity.

Sandra said, "Oh honey, you aren't a people pleaser. You have a different problem, I have seen this many times before. You are serving a false idol, the idol of independence. Your issue is that you have elevated your own independence to a place of honor that is not Godly. You are afraid of yielding your own independence and freedom to your future husband. You have to tear the idol down." Then she prayed for me.

Back then, my discernment wasn't what it is today, and what she said sounded really spiritual. I swallowed this counsel hook, line, and sinker. After all, Sandra was on staff at a prominent Christian organization that had solid teaching, and I was still learning the ways of the Holy Spirit. I think a big part of me was also relieved I wouldn't have to disappoint Kevin by breaking up with him. It was a lot easier for me to believe that I had an obligation to be less independent and needed to yield more to Kevin rather than believe my primary problem was being a people pleaser with no sense of my own boundaries. Instead of stepping out of the curse in the garden, I stepped back into it. My desire would be for my husband, and he would rule over me. Ironically, the real idol in this situation wasn't my independence, but it was Kevin.

I didn't go back again to Donna the counselor. Instead, I set out to tear the "idol" down. I needed to love unconditionally, put myself aside, and learn to submit to others including Kevin, to stop being so independent. I needed to put my needs second and others first, especially him. For the six months following this, all the things that I now know were red flags in my relationship with Kevin (who quickly became my fiancé), were brushed away as symptoms of my idol of independence. This was something that was my weakness, my problem, and I needed to deal with it. I thought God was teaching me something. I didn't realize I had again partnered with religion, works, and obligation instead of God. I was falling straight into the trap the enemy had laid for me to drag me back into captivity.

In premarital counseling at our church, the primary focus was on me. Kevin was now the executive pastor on staff, and everyone loved him. We focused a lot on making sure I was healthy enough to get married again. What about my relationship with my mother? Was I healed from my previous divorce? My pastor encouraged me to ensure my vows included the phrase, "I will never consider a divorce," because divorce is not Biblical.

At this point, I hope you are screaming to these pages, "Don't do it! Don't marry him!" But as I said earlier, dysfunctional behavioral patterns that aren't addressed will always keep repeating themselves. Donna had done her best to steer me toward some authentic identity in Christ and addressing people-pleasing tendencies, but the enemy had other plans. That curse from the fall was in full force in my life: I was a weak-willed woman being manipulated by the devil, with a desire for her husband who would rule over her. I was sucked back into a cycle of religious obligation where I traded authentic connection for works and trying to be good enough. And this was a pretty comfortable situation for me—it felt normal.

Most people were fully on board with me marrying Kevin, but I dismissed the few who unsuccessfully tried to intervene. Our young adult pastor came to me with concerns that Kevin would be offended if my professional career was more successful or my spiritual calling was more visible than Kevin's. A friend and her mother pulled me aside and told me they were really uncomfortable how Kevin made so many jokes and jabs at my expense, and they could tell it hurt me. But I had relinquished all my choices that day in Pennsylvania when I determined to tear the idol down by submitting to Kevin.

So I married him.

JUST GO TO SLEEP

I had been married to Kevin for about a year when my friend, Annie, came to visit. Annie was on staff with the well-known healing evangelist who had prophesied over me, and she was there during my "great awakening." I planned on hosting my first family Thanksgiving the week following her visit, so we made a "practice" turkey with all the fixings. We laughed until we cried learning how to use a Neti Pot and trying to remove ear wax with ear candles (not recommended).

CHAPTER FIVE: BACK INTO BONDAGE

Toward the end of her visit, Annie pulled me aside and asked if we could go for a drive alone together. As we backed out of the driveway and drove up my street, she said: "Why do you let Kevin treat you like that?"

I had no earthly idea what she was talking about. I said, "What do you mean?"

"He tells you what to do and not do. He criticizes you constantly. Your cooking isn't right. Your comments are invalid. Your outfits embarrass him. Your ideas are picked apart and shot down. Is this kind of thing normal in your relationship?"

I was dumbfounded. Part of me felt like I was supposed to defend Kevin. But Annie had opened a small window of fresh air in a dark and smoky house. "Yes," I said. "This is normal."

"You've got to talk to him about this," Annie said. "It's not okay."

So after she left, I brought it up with Kevin.

"Did Annie tell you to talk to me about this?" he asked.

"Well, she made some observations, and I think they are important. It's true that you sometimes do these things." I tried to use words like "I feel" instead of making sharp accusations. I said, "I feel hurt when you constantly shoot down my thoughts and ideas. I feel wounded by your unkind comments about my clothes and my cooking. I don't feel affection from you, and I feel alone in this relationship." It felt good to say these things to him out loud. Why had I been stuffing it all down?

The confrontation escalated. Kevin called Annie unkind names and announced she wasn't welcome in our home anymore because she was "driving a wedge between us." I cried, because he refused to acknowledge any possibility that he had done something wrong. I cried because I wanted Annie to be allowed back. Then I yelled, because I realized how hurt I actually was, and he didn't seem to care. He said, "Look how you're acting. You're being crazy. You need to get control of yourself." I went to bed completely exhausted and he went to watch TV. I thought, if I "just go to sleep," maybe this will blow over in the morning.

When I woke up the next day, my eyes were so puffy from crying they were almost swollen shut. I put on extra makeup and my glasses, making myself as presentable as possible. I had just been promoted again at work, and as one of the youngest rising executives at my company— a global, publicly traded Fortune 500—I really needed to focus. I stuffed all my feelings down and pushed through the day.

Over the years that followed, I lived in an endless cycle. The cycle looked like this: I would reach a boiling point from Kevin's cruelty. I would confront him for treating me poorly. I would give examples. He would deny any responsibility and blame me for his behavior. He would tell me I could help by giving more to our sexual relationship or by being more self-sacrificing in other ways. I would cry. He would say my expectations were too high. He would refuse to go to a marriage counselor. I would become angry, and yell. He would call me crazy and over-emotional, and say I have anger issues. I would go to bed with eyes swollen from crying and voice hoarse from yelling, and he would go watch TV. I would "just go to sleep" and wake up the next day and go to work, where I couldn't be an emotional disaster, so I stuffed it all down, again.

HAVING KIDS DOESN'T CHANGE A CRUEL MAN

I was completely miserable in my marriage to Kevin, but completely in denial about it. In my mind, this was a lifetime commitment, where I had vowed to never consider divorcing. When Kevin refused to get counseling or to take any level of ownership, I tried to focus on work and church and to keep hoping that eventually God would get through to him and we could be happy. I never acknowledged in my own heart that I was in constant, unending emotional pain. I didn't want to live as a victim, and I thought acknowledging my pain would make me one. I wanted to be strong.

It seems cheesy, and everyone says never to do this, but I believed having children with Kevin might soften him and make him remember to be a good role model, as well as make things better in our marriage. As dysfunctional as it was, I hoped if I gave him a son like he wanted, that he might actually be kind to me. And I had always wanted children.

I got pregnant right away when we started trying. And I absolutely loved being pregnant. I cooked and froze endless meals to prepare. I cleaned everything in a "nesting" frenzy, focusing my full attention on getting ready for this baby boy, performing at work, continuing to provide our primary income through my salary, and hoping for a brighter future.

Someone gave Kevin their "best" parenting advice: that two sleep-deprived parents were worse than one, and that the man wasn't much help in the middle of the night anyway if the mother was nursing. And so we began our parenting journey on that note. Kevin didn't miss a wink of sleep. In fact, Kevin had a skill for never being inconvenienced in any way as a parent.

I adored my twelve weeks of maternity leave but I was ready to return to work when the time came. I loved being a mother, but I loved working, too. I loved the problem solving, the strategic thinking, the teamwork and camaraderie, and the challenges of global business. I felt God's presence and anointing with me in the workplace, and it felt good. At work, I was allowed to have opinions and to operate in my gifts. It was the only place where I could actually be who I really was.

So our lives continued on, now as parents. And where before I was taking care of myself and Kevin's needs full time, now I was also taking care of our child, and then two years later, one more son.

I would never consider my children a difficulty or burden, and I am so grateful God chose me to be their mom. But those years with Kevin, they were fully my responsibility. I would get them both ready for preschool, get myself ready for work, pack their lunches, take them to school, go to work all day, then pick them up, drive home in traffic, make dinner for everyone, clean up after everyone, give the kids baths, tuck them into bed, and then fall into bed, exhausted. I was a one-man-band. And Kevin wasn't more kind to me as I had hoped. He wasn't kind at all. I was still very alone, just more busy and alone.

LOVE AND RESPECT

Our church scheduled a marriage workshop based on a book called *Love and Respect*. Because Kevin was a pastor at our church, we were obligated to attend. But I didn't feel obligated, I was actually thrilled at this opportunity. I was willing to do whatever it took to make our marriage work, even if it was hard. I prayed that this would be a catalyst for us, and that we would navigate together into a healthier season in our relationship.

The foundational premise of *Love and Respect* was simple: that a woman has one driving need, (to be loved) and a man has one driving need (to be respected). Therefore, when the woman felt loved, she would be happy in the marriage, and when a man felt respected, he would be happy in the marriage. But when these needs (love and respect) were not met in a relationship, couples could fall into cycles of dysfunction. This means that a wife who doesn't feel loved can have trouble offering respect to her husband, and in the same way, a husband who doesn't feel respected can have trouble offering love to his wife.

This really resonated with me. I completely agreed that my most basic need in my marriage to Kevin was to be loved. I needed to feel seen and to be cared for, to receive affection from him, and for him to be nice to me.

But if this was all true—and I wasn't feeling loved—could the issue be that I wasn't respecting Kevin, that he didn't feel respected by me?

After the workshop, Kevin was excited. He said to me, "This is exactly what I've been feeling all along. You don't respect me."

I think I saw this one coming. I racked my brain to catalog my interactions with him, to find a place where I disrespected him somehow. I already constantly deferred to him in decision making. I already smothered my own opinions when he had different ones and didn't want to hear any other points of view. I already waited on him hand and foot, trying to anticipate his needs—what he wanted for dinner, what he wanted to do on weekends, what he wanted to see at the movies, or how he wanted to decorate the house. I continued to financially provide for our family and paid for him to have the brand new car he wanted. I was willing to change, but I couldn't think of a single area in our relationship that he could possibly feel disrespected by me. I had no idea how much I had already purposefully made myself small so he could feel big.

I asked if he could give some examples of how I could respect him more or some examples of how he felt disrespected. He didn't have any examples. He said something like, "You don't need examples, you already know what I'm talking about." I didn't know at all. The despair I felt in that moment was completely crushing. I had no path forward, no plan to grow a healthy marriage, no things to work on, no idea what to do. I am pretty sure that is when I started drinking.

NUMBING

I didn't realize I was drinking to numb my pain, but that's exactly what it was. The pain of my life was too much to bear. I wanted a reprieve from the torment of everyday life, the torment of never being good enough and not being cared for, the torment of feeling trapped in a jail made by my own choices.

I grew up in a house where drinking was generally frowned upon. As a rebellious teenager, I drank a few times and ended up vomiting. In Christian college, drinking was not allowed and in order to attend, you had to sign an agreement you wouldn't drink, socially dance, and/or have premarital sex.

I didn't dump my extra-religious philosophy on drinking until after my post-Henry "great awakening." I came to enjoy a glass of wine with my parents every so often. I stopped judging occasional wine drinkers as the spawn of Satan. I respected those who chose not to drink, and I respected those who chose not to have rigid rules about it.

But now, in this life with Kevin, and the crushing pressure of his expectations, my job, being our family's primary provider, and our now two small children—for whom I was the sole caretaker—I started having something to drink every single night. Then I started having two somethings to drink every single night. Years went by, without going a single night without one or two somethings to drink. I managed my pain with a nightly routine where my heart pain could be temporarily numbed. I wasn't getting drunk…just taking the edge of the pain off.

After we had been married a few years, my dad pulled me aside at a family event. He was so angry, his hands shook. He said he was done listening to Kevin talk to me that way—dismissing my opinions, and making fun of me with cutting sarcasm. He was not going to stand for it anymore. I told my dad that I needed to pick my battles and there would be negative consequences for me if he brought it up. We would probably stop coming to family events. So Dad reluctantly backed down, because I asked him to. And I grabbed another cocktail.

Looking back, I'm really glad I didn't get into pain pills, pornography, affairs, or some other horrid coping mechanism in my marriage to Kevin. Not that over-drinking wasn't wrong, but I could have really destroyed my mind and body in some very bad ways. Even in that dark season, God was there, keeping the wheels on the bus, keeping me from going off the deep end, and keeping my future and hope intact no matter what. But it was a dark season indeed.

HOPE DEFERRED

I'm a pretty positive, joyful, optimistic person. Like many other people pleasers, hope, faith, and seeing the best in people are some of my greatest strengths. So I constantly looked forward to life changes that might shift things for Kevin and make him happier so we could have a strong marriage. After all, I reminded myself of this scripture:

"Love…bears all things, believes all things, hopes all things, endures all things" (1 Corinthians 13:7, NKJV).

Kevin was really unhappy as Executive Pastor at our church. He believed the church should be run differently. He was miserable every day. Every night he would talk about how upset he was about the unqualified people he worked with. I thought leaving the church might make things better. Even though I now led the worship team once or twice a month, and I knew that worship and music were a big part of God's plan for me, I couldn't bear the dark storm cloud that had settled over our life. Kevin resigned, and we left the church—and we didn't go back to church after that.

Kevin was out of work for a while after he quit. But the dark storm cloud over our life didn't leave, it just changed and darkened. Now the source of every day's grumpy mood was him being out of work. He applied and interviewed for a few roles he didn't get, and this devastated him. I was on an emotional roller coaster with him. I prayed, but my selfish prayers

CHAPTER FIVE: BACK INTO BONDAGE

were focused on him getting a job so he would be happy so I wouldn't have so much pain. I hoped that his finding a new job would change things.

He finally found a job in the career field he wanted. The job was great at first, but after a while, Kevin became miserable again. He thought incompetent people were in leadership positions. He believed he was being grossly underpaid compared to others. He wanted to be better recognized for his skills, like so-and-so. He came home every day with a whole new set of criticisms for his co-workers. He started talking about looking for a new job again. The dark storm cloud over our life was worse than ever. I hoped if he changed jobs again, maybe then things would take a turn for the better.

We decided that moving to California, where all his family lived, was the next step. I thought perhaps the "spiritual climate" of where we lived was part of the problem. I thought for sure a new job and new town and being around his family would bring a breakthrough and that things would begin to improve. I took a tremendous risk moving to California, because I was now one of the youngest vice presidents at my company. But by the grace of God, things at work were okay. I was hoping we were starting a brand new season, in a new state, with a new house, and with his family around. I prayed for the shift to finally come.

Kevin had a long commute for his new job, and he hated that. Beyond the commute, he thought he wasn't getting promoted fast enough, and he believed he was overqualified for his job. So, he found a new job, where he worked from home. We sat in the same office working from home. Rather than having my own space to do my work and lead my team, I now had him there, telling me to stop loudly drinking coffee, shushing me when I got too animated for his taste on conference calls, and critiquing my behavior constantly. For years, work had been the only place I was allowed to be strong, assertive, and important. But now I had Kevin there in the office with his meanness every day, telling me everything I did that displeased him. No, things in California did not improve. With every change and every year, and especially moving to California, our relationship got worse...so much worse.

I had no idea the curse had repeated itself again in my life: the curse of sin that I was born into, the curse of being weak-willed and ruled by a man, the curse of falling into a deep, dark hole of religious obligation that made me believe I had no choices. I was completely trapped. I had vowed to not divorce. And we now had two precious boys, five and seven years old, and I didn't want to mess up their lives.

CHAPTER FIVE: BACK INTO BONDAGE

QUESTIONS FOR THE READER:

1. Even if you are married, do you have a list of things that are important qualities of your spouse? Are you in touch with the things you authentically need in a relationship?

2. Do you see patterns of people pleasing in your own life? Where?

3. Have you received bad counsel that has derailed you from the right path and sent you into a season of captivity to the enemy's strategies? Do you look to God for leadership and direction, or has your spouse become your idol?

4. Are you self-medicating your heart pain with numbing coping mechanisms like drinking, taking prescription narcotics or sleeping pills, or even escaping in things like books or TV?

5. Are you living in a season of hope deferred? What keeps you there?

READ THIS PRAYER OUT LOUD:

Holy Spirit, thank you for being near to me, for being closer than a brother, for being a constant help in times of trouble. I ask that you would come with your kindness and power, to meet me in the season I am in. I ask that you would show me places of people pleasing, where I have lost connection to my own heart and needs, and am operating in an unhealthy over-focus on doing what others expect and being what others need at the sacrifice of my own personhood. I ask that you would reveal to me places where I've received bad counsel not aligned with the Spirit of God. I ask that you would reveal places where I'm numbing my pain in an effort to survive my life. God of the universe, thank you that you see me, care about me, and are able to rescue me from every place of captivity I'm living in. Right now, I surrender all my fears: fear of disappointing others, fear of the unknown, fear of the religious accusations of others, and fear of not being good enough. I accept the grace and love you offer in exchange for my fear. Thank you Jesus that you promised to never leave me and that you promised to walk with me until the very end. I believe you made me for freedom, not for captivity, and that you are able to make all things new in my life. I ask for wisdom, revelation, power, counsel, discernment, and peace as you take me by the hand and lead me into new life. I declare that I am returning to the garden: to the place God made me—of perfect union with the Father and perfect identity as a mirror image of himself.

Chapter Six

LIVING IN THE CURSE: EMOTIONAL ABUSE AND NARCISSISM

*Your desire shall be for your husband,
and he shall rule over you.*
Genesis 3:16b (NKJV)

PHIL AND JUDY

The day I had coffee with Claire and I woke up, everything changed.

After nearly a decade, I wasn't asleep anymore. And it was terrifying. I needed help.

I went to the garage, sat in my car, and called Phil and Judy, who were parent-type figures to me and Kevin. They had been at our wedding, and occasionally we would meet them for dinner. They were Spirit-filled and a great source of wisdom, and lived nearby.

Thankfully when I called, Phil and Judy were in their car together and they put me on speakerphone. I told them I wasn't okay and that I was not going to pretend anymore. I told them I had almost ten years of stuffed-down pain from Kevin coming to the surface. I told them I was afraid—afraid this would end in divorce, afraid of wounding my children, afraid of making the wrong choices.

In that moment, I was most terrified that Phil and Judy were going to tell me that I needed to make a commitment to stay with Kevin no matter what. I was afraid they were going to tell me that I had to keep praying for him until he finally changed. I was afraid a religious spirit of condemnation would tell me that I must remain small, silent, compliant, and suffering because it was what God expected from me. And I wanted out of that painful life.

Frankly, I was afraid of being in pain forever, because Kevin wasn't changing. It would have been better to stay numb, with a heart frozen in ice while self-medicating with two cocktails a night, than to face all this pain, only to have it continue for the rest of my life.

Phil and Judy did not respond in the religious way I feared. They told me they loved me and they had seen how Kevin treated me over the years. They prayed for me, for wisdom and strength. They offered to let me come and stay with them, but I was not leaving my children (I could only imagine what Kevin would do if I tried to take them to live somewhere else). I needed to stay put.

And then Judy asked me, "Have you read any books on emotional abuse?"

"No," I said. I didn't know what emotional abuse was.

EMOTIONAL ABUSE

I didn't remember ever hearing the term "emotional abuse" before. They don't exactly teach general education classes in college on this. Physical abuse is one thing, it's super obvious because it leaves behind physical marks, but emotional abuse? It sounded kind-of fluffy to me. But after Judy recommended a book on the subject (and I quickly devoured it), the more I read, the more I knew this was exactly what had been going on in my relationship with Kevin for the last nine-and-a-half years. I was also pretty sure it was a big part of the problem in my first marriage to Henry.

"Abuse" is a big scary word that shouldn't be taken lightly. There are two kinds of abuse: physical and emotional (also known as psychological). I think it would be hard to argue about whether physical abuse is actually abuse—we can probably all agree it is. But "emotional abuse" was exactly the kind of term that Kevin would have despised. He would have made fun of it and called it a crutch for victims to stay victims. He would have rolled his eyes and called it psychological hocus-pocus.

I know some women whose families disowned them because they got divorced on the grounds of emotional abuse from their spouse. Some well-intending Christians have a "zero tolerance" policy when it comes to divorce when the offending spouse hasn't committed adultery or engaged in physical abuse. While this topic is interesting, for now, to divorce or not divorce is not the primary issue. For now, we need to understand something foundational—what exactly is emotional abuse?

Let's start with the basic definition of abuse. Abuse is using something or someone for a purpose it was not created or intended for. When someone becomes addicted to pain medications and can't live without them,

CHAPTER SIX: LIVING IN THE CURSE: EMOTIONAL ABUSE AND NARCISSISM

it's called drug abuse because the medicine wasn't created to be used in that way. Slavery is abuse because humans were not created to be trapped against their will in unconditional service to other humans. Human trafficking is abuse because humans were not created to be stolen and used physically for the pleasure of others. Sexually taking advantage of a child is abuse because a child was not created to be used sexually by anyone. Similarly, emotional abuse is abuse because humans were not intended to be enslaved or tortured through others' control and manipulation.

Building upon the definition of "abuse," here is the definition of "emotional abuse" from the American Psychological Association:

> *Also called psychological abuse, emotional abuse is non-physical abuse, a pattern of behavior in which one person deliberately and repeatedly subjects another to non-physical acts that are detrimental to behavioral and affective functioning and overall mental well-being. Researchers have yet to formulate a universally agreed-upon definition of the concept, but they have identified a variety of forms that emotional abuse may take, including verbal abuse; intimidation and terrorization; humiliation and degradation; exploitation; harassment; rejection and withholding of affection; isolation and excessive control.*

If you think about the curse of the fall in Genesis 3 ("your desire shall be for your husband, and he shall rule over you"), this sounds about right. Of course not every man is emotionally abusive and feels the need to "rule" their wives. In the same way, not every area of the curse applies to all people at all times. But it stands to reason that one of the most devastating, broadly occurring patterns resulting from the curse and the fall is the pattern of emotional abuse, where women believe they must comply with the men who rule over them. The emotional abuse of women by men with narcissistic traits is a direct result from the fall and has been a common pattern in every generation since the beginning of time. The pride of men leads them to seek to rule over women, and the religion of women leads them to conform and comply because they think it's required.

The first big step in my "freedom process" was waking up and actually acknowledging something was really wrong in my marriage and believing it was not all my fault. For years, I knew something was wrong, but I believed the lie that I had the personal power to change it, by being better, doing better, or trying harder. Don't get me wrong: it certainly takes two to have a dysfunctional marriage. And it's clear that my lifetime patterns of people pleasing, living out of religious obligation, and becoming small, silent, and compliant in an effort to protect myself from pain inflicted by the cruel people around me were all issues I owned. However, no woman ever exits lifetime patterns of abusive relationships until they actually recognize they have been abused.

I had to come to terms with the fact that how I was treated by Kevin wasn't just mistreatment, but very serious emotional abuse. The reason this was hard for me was because I didn't want to be a victim. I didn't want to be a whiny, complaining, pitiful abused woman who was weak and feeling sorry for herself. But again, it is impossible to find freedom from cycles of emotional abuse without firmly acknowledging what it is. If we minimize it or dismiss it, we minimize the need and importance of finding the root, breaking the pattern, and getting fully healed. We must see it fully for what it is. Abuse is never acceptable…it is always from hell itself.

Obviously, moving beyond the stage of realizing you've been abused is important, and we will deal with that process, too (the great news is - you don't have to be a victim!). But failing to recognize abuse is one of the fastest ways to guarantee you will find yourself back in another abusive situation. Look at my story: I married Henry, who had narcissistic tendencies, belittled and ignored me; then I moved on to Mauricio, who seemed great at first, but manipulated and controlled me by spying on me using astral projection objects; and before I was able to address the root of these patterns with Donna the counselor, I was sucked into my deepest and darkest captivity through my marriage with Kevin.

IS IT ABUSE?

That said, we do need to get more specific about "what is emotional abuse." Perhaps you're like I was, and have been living in abuse for many years without realizing it. Perhaps you know someone in a situation like this,

CHAPTER SIX: LIVING IN THE CURSE: EMOTIONAL ABUSE AND NARCISSISM

and you need the confidence to help wake them up. Perhaps you're a pastor or leader who needs more tools to identify red flags in couples to ensure you're not endorsing relationships headed for disaster. In any case, emotional abuse is one of the most secret, silent killers of women in the world, and is a lot more common than physical abuse. In order to recognize emotional abuse, and ultimately stop the cycle, we must first understand how it looks. So to that end: in my story, emotional abuse manifested in ten different ways.

1- He blamed me for his mistreatment.

Psychologists call this "gaslighting." It's the form of emotional abuse where the abuser never takes responsibility for his wrongdoing, but blames his behavior and its bad impacts on his partner. Adam was the first to do this. He blamed his sin on Eve.

This form of abuse was present in every cycle of confrontation between Kevin and me. I would confront him for his mistreatment, and he would cite all the reasons why I caused his behavior.

When I would periodically confront him for the way he treated me, he often blamed my lack of spending quality time with him as (what he believed to be) the real issue. When I asked what kind of quality time he wanted, he would say he wanted me to sit with him on the couch after the kids went to bed, and watch his favorite TV shows with him, not talking, and without my phone. He wanted this even though it wasn't actually quality time at all—him watching TV that I didn't want to watch and me just sitting there without interacting—when I was usually dead tired from a long day at work (and from doing all family and household duties alone).

Kevin would also blame his cruelty toward me on the fact that I didn't meet his needs sexually. He would say things like, "You know that for men, our moods are based on how much our physical needs are being met. If you would give more to me physically, it would put me in a better mood."

Kevin would get really grouchy and mean when he didn't like what I wore because it called attention to me. "You know I don't like it when you dress up. If you would wear something else, I wouldn't be so upset." He actually blamed his mistreatment of me on the clothes I chose to wear.

After years of being blamed for every part of our dysfunctional marriage, I suppose it wasn't a surprise that I actually believed—until Claire woke me up—that I <u>was</u> completely to blame.

2 - There was never a good time to talk about things.

Men who emotionally abuse their partners almost never want to have a talk about their relationship, especially if it puts them in a position to be criticized in any way.

Kevin would never agree to couples counseling, and neither did he ever want to talk one-on-one about our relationship. He would do anything to avoid these kinds of conversations, including hurling insults at me and getting me angry, subsequently pointing out how I was an angry person. I believe he avoided counseling because he was afraid someone would see and call out how sick and frail he actually was.

I never found the right time or the right way to bring things up. If I did it calmly and peacefully or if I did it in an angry, emotional rage, it made no difference. Kevin did not want to have a relationship discussion under any circumstances.

When Kevin was in a foul mood, the worst thing I could ever do was to ask or talk about it. He would say, "You know you always make it worse when you bring it up." He made it impossible to discuss our marriage and relationship in any constructive way. I was conditioned by Kevin to not bring issues up, because when I did, there was always a backlash against me.

Once or twice, I got the great idea that Kevin and I should read our vows to each other again, or to watch our wedding video together. He refused and made it clear how much the thought disgusted him. Asking him to talk or do something that connected us emotionally was always risky, because of the rejection that routinely followed.

3 - He made it hard to have friends and connections.

I didn't find out until after I woke up and made some phone calls to friends back home that many of them had stopped calling us or hanging out with us because no one wanted to deal with Kevin's moods. Some friends noticed Kevin would pout and brood when the conversation didn't focus entirely on him.

I don't blame these couples for not wanting to be around us, and hanging out with other couples was something we didn't do very often. But what was even more infrequent was me hanging out with girlfriends one-on-one.

Year after year, Kevin resisted and criticized my female friendships. The only ones he would tolerate were the ones who really liked him, engaged him, and even admired him. You already know I was prohibited from continuing my friendship with Annie, because she noticed Kevin's bad behavior after our first year of marriage and she encouraged me to address it. In fact, anyone I befriended who was assertive, strong, or confident, Kevin would immediately despise. Interestingly, I can't think of a single "strong" woman, either in our personal life or a public figure, whom Kevin didn't despise.

I let most of my female connections fizzle out because it was too hard to try to maintain them. Kevin would get irritated if I was on the phone, and if I wanted to spend time with friends, he would either refuse because it would eat in on "our family time" or he would insist the kids go with me, because he didn't want to "watch them." This kind of isolation, where it is impossible to maintain friendships, is a form of emotional abuse.

Before we moved to California, Kevin would look for every possible reason to avoid holidays, birthdays, or get-togethers with my extended family, who were all local. He would say how uncomfortable he was and he would suggest alternate plans. He also constantly criticized my parents and my sister and her husband, and it made it difficult to spend time with them. In short, being with anyone from my family was a painful struggle, and over time we did less and less of it.

When we moved to California for Kevin's job, I left my entire family behind. A major indicator of emotional abuse is when the abuser isolates their spouse from any independent support system.

4 - He limited my personal freedom.

I grew up with a great love for music and a great joy in singing. Music is one of the great joys of my heart. I know that I was made to worship, it is part of the fabric of my soul.

I had received three significant prophetic words about singing and playing keyboard when I first discovered the Holy Spirit. I knew that part of my God-given calling was to sing, worship, and play with all my heart. When I first met Kevin, my musical inclinations never seemed to be a problem.

After we had our first son, when we still attended a local church, Kevin began to get upset when I had to leave for worship team practice and he had to stay with the baby. And let's be clear— I love being a mother and I would do anything for my children—they were never and will never be a burden or a task to me. But I couldn't take my little one to loud band practice, and Kevin started to voice his irritation at my occasional need (once or twice a month) to leave the baby behind for an hour or two.

I had an old keyboard, but it didn't work very well. On one of my birthdays, Kevin gifted me a piano. This piano was a surprise, and I was really excited. I didn't mind that it was old, out of tune, and that he got it for next to nothing on Craig's List—I was just excited he seemed to be supporting me in my musical pursuits.

I'm pretty sure Kevin quickly regretted this. Looking back, he gifted it to me when we had visitors from out of town, and he got a lot of accolades from them for this gift choice; perhaps this was part of his motivation. He soon asked me to not play or sing unless he was gone. And he was only gone for work, which was the same time I was gone for work.

The piano sat unused. I didn't play or sing because I didn't want to be reprimanded for being annoying and I didn't want to be told to be quiet—the piano was on the same floor of our house as the TV. He used subtle control and punishment to keep me from doing the one thing my heart needed.

Besides the fights I would have with Kevin when I had to travel for work, the second most frequent cause for conflict between us was when I went for walks.

CHAPTER SIX: LIVING IN THE CURSE: EMOTIONAL ABUSE AND NARCISSISM

If I were you and reading this, I would have a hard time believing that going for walks could possibly be a "top cause" for conflict in any marriage. But in our case, it was. Being alone on a walk was the only time, other than work travel, that I could spend with the Lord. I longed for the time I could sing, pray, and cry, and ask the Lord to come into my life, to take me out of the winter season. Perhaps the dark spiritual forces that ruled Kevin knew this, and it's why my walks were such a problem. I had to basically beg and negotiate to go. The only time it wasn't a problem for him was when he was gone to work—but I had to work, too.

5 - He insisted I meet his needs - including sexually.

Why is this in the category of emotional abuse and not physical sexual abuse? The American Psychological Association defines sexual abuse as "unwanted sexual activity, with perpetrators using force, making threats, or taking advantage of victims not able to give consent."

What happened in my relationship sexually with Kevin was never him physically forcing himself upon me, and I did consent. However, he made it clear to me that if he was not satisfied sexually, that his moods would worsen. And it was true—whenever I avoided sexual interaction with him (because it was not enjoyable for me, but something I dreaded), he would point to that as the reason for his moods. In this way, he used control and manipulation to ensure his sexual needs would be fulfilled, and to ensure that I would not protest.

When I was married to Kevin, it felt like my entire life was about keeping him satisfied so he would not turn his unkind wrath toward me. His moods would always lead to cruelty toward me, and I would do almost anything to avoid the pain of his sharp words. You may recall from the story of when Claire woke me up that I told her that I hadn't kissed Kevin on the lips for several years. That might give you an insight into our physical relationship. I was not an active participant in him getting what he "needed." I might have been there physically, but mentally and emotionally I was completely detached. I had to disconnect my heart from my body in order to bear it.

I am not sure there is anything more violating than someone using your body to give themselves pleasure without regard for you as a person. Over the course of many years, my sexual dignity was eroded to nothing.

6 - He wanted me to stay small and not draw attention to myself.

Only a truly insecure person tries to keep someone else small so they can feel big. And only someone who has been habitually abused will intentionally try to remain small to try to manage someone else's insecurity.

It's interesting that before I married Kevin, I had quite a skill and growling demand for me to do public speaking engagements and press interviews at work. I had traveled extensively in this capacity—to Barcelona, South Africa, Mexico City, Madrid, Macau, Paris, London, and elsewhere. I had been interviewed and quoted in industry publications as an expert in my professional field. But that abruptly ended when Kevin and I married. At first, he positioned it as wanting to spend time together as a married couple. But as we had one and then two children, my leaving town for something not critical for my job was no longer an option. And speaking engagements weren't exactly critical.

While Kevin and I were married, I only had one speaking engagement during a period of nine years, and it was a presentation to a women's executive network at a nearby large corporation. I prepared very carefully for this speaking engagement, as I always do. I wanted to dig deep inside and bring out some personal, insightful nuggets of truth that could really help women succeed in being both mothers and executives. I got a lot of great feedback about my presentation from those in attendance, and when I shared the video recording link with others, I had several women tell me how it was actually life-changing for them.

When I asked Kevin if he watched it, his reply was, "I watched a few minutes, then I sort-of skipped through. It was hard to watch." I never expected accolades from Kevin, but this one hurt. He was not excited about the prospect of me being elevated in any way.

Perhaps more painful than Kevin's reaction to my women's executive network speaking engagement was how embarrassed he became when I dressed up—or more accurately, when I wore basically anything besides yoga pants or plain jeans. He encouraged me to wear things that were as

CHAPTER SIX: LIVING IN THE CURSE: EMOTIONAL ABUSE AND NARCISSISM

inconspicuous as possible. I've thought a lot about where he was coming from in his desire for me to always "dress down." In the end, I think he was worried about being compared to me. I think he was worried that someone would have one perspective of me based on my attire, and a different, lesser perspective of him, based on what he wore. The root was insecurity.

Our last Christmas as a married couple, we were invited to a large holiday party hosted by his employer. It was a formal event, where people really dressed up. The company spared no expense on venue, entertainment, and food.

I bought a stunning, black velvet one-shouldered dress for this event. It was classy, simple, and flattering. The night of the event, Kevin tried for an hour to talk me into wearing something more plain. He pulled out a few dresses I had worn to work on a regular basis and begged me to wear one of them. I refused. I didn't want to wear something meant for routine business meetings when the event dress code was cocktail party attire.

Because I didn't change my outfit, Kevin hardly spoke to me all night. He didn't speak to me on the drive there, he didn't interact with me at the event, and when his colleagues would compliment him on "his beautiful wife," he would become embarrassed and change the subject. It's hard for me to believe that he was embarrassed because he thought I didn't look good. More likely, he was embarrassed because he was afraid people would compare us.

The other time this kind of abuse would manifest was when we were with other people and the discussion centered on me and not him. Kevin was deeply envious and insecure about my professional achievements. In retrospect, Kevin had also conditioned my family to ensure the conversation orbited around him. I think everyone was wary of his tendency to pout, and we all walked on eggshells to ensure he felt important and celebrated in every conversation to avoid "grumpy Kevin." It was exhausting for everyone involved and a very manipulative dynamic. My sister later told me that she still can't believe how Kevin "had us all trained" to talk about how great he was, even when he wasn't there. I didn't realize how much my family was also impacted by Kevin's abuse.

7 - He was proud of me only when it made him look good, and he took my achievements as his own.

By the eighth year of our marriage, I became the youngest vice president in my company at the time. My professional accomplishments at my global, publicly traded employer were not insignificant. I was the person they often called upon for difficult, high-stakes assignments. In fact, I never held a job that someone had before me—all my roles were first-time roles, created to solve hard business problems, and several with reporting responsibility to our public board of directors or with public visibility.

That year, I got a call from my CEO asking if I would join a small, hand-picked team of executives focused on transforming the organization and driving long-term growth. The two-year assignment would be an incredible opportunity for my career. This invitation said a lot about my company's confidence in me and their views of my potential.

Kevin was angry. He was concerned this might mean more travel for me, that instead of an average of one business trip per month I might have...two? I told him this was not the kind of opportunity you decline if you want to continue to work somewhere and succeed. I accepted the assignment, without the support of my spouse. Like many things in our marriage, I did it alone.

Kevin would never speak about being proud of me or about my career success. He would, however, speak freely to others about "our success." He loved when members of his family would call us a "power couple." When our financial advisor would come over once per year, he would act as if all the earnings—which were over two thirds from my income, were hard-earned by him.

There was nothing in my heart that needed to be recognized, praised, or acknowledged as the primary breadwinner for my family. I wasn't angry about how Kevin wouldn't give me any credit. But looking back, I can see how his taking my achievements as his own was wrong - it was abusive.

8 - He withheld affection and was indifferent to my needs and my heart.

I always knew my dad loved me. I knew because of his kindness, his eagerness to hear about my life, even the softness toward me in his eyes.

CHAPTER SIX: LIVING IN THE CURSE: EMOTIONAL ABUSE AND NARCISSISM

His hug was such a safe place. I knew he would overlook any mistake I made. He saw my potential. He believed in me big time.

My first husband, Henry, didn't show love for me. It was like giving me affection was too costly and made him vulnerable.

I think Kevin tried hard to be kind to me when we were dating. But it was still a red flag, even then. I remember saying to him when we were engaged, "The most important thing to me is that you are nice to me." He promised he would be. I truly was afraid of another Henry situation, and indeed, it became one.

When Kevin and I were engaged, we went to the wedding of a couple we knew. Their connection was so real, tender, and kind. Their vows were gentle, raw, and open-hearted. I remember crying my eyes out through their entire ceremony, unable to stop. Back then, being out of touch with my own feelings, I had no idea what was wrong with me or why I was even crying. I didn't realize the reason I cried was because the affection and love that existed in their relationship was missing from mine with Kevin. An intense mourning rose from my heart, and I could not stop it.

Kevin only touched me when he wanted to have sex. And then, it wasn't the tender kind of touch I really needed.

Kevin didn't dance with me. He made fun of me and told the kids I danced like a Muppet, which was kind-of funny, but was also just mean sarcasm at my expense. At weddings and events where there was dancing, even couples slow dancing, he refused to dance with me. I danced with the old people or the kids.

Kevin never said anything kind. When I would call from overseas on a work trip, he would sit silent on the line. I would ask questions and try to connect or tell him about my day, and he would be non-responsive. I assumed it was because he was punishing me for traveling.

I could not watch romantic movies. Seeing a man treat a woman with kindness and tenderness was agony.

When I would try to communicate with Kevin about my need to receive affection and be told I was loved, his usual response was to accuse me of being insecure and to point out I should just believe, and not need to hear or see evidence that he loved me.

Being in a relationship where you've pledged your life to a person who withholds all affection is a terrible kind of torment. It's abusive.

9 - He believed he was right and I was wrong, and constantly told me.

Kevin loved talking about his ideas, thoughts, and opinions, but had a zero tolerance policy for any ideas, thoughts, and opinions of mine, especially if they were about spiritual things. Because he was always right, he never, ever, apologized.

Over the years, I almost completely stopped saying what I thought at home, because each time I expressed an opinion about something, Kevin was sure to come back with a response that invalidated my views. He equated a difference of opinion as "disrespect" toward him. In our relationship, I was not permitted to exhibit assertiveness. If I was even slightly assertive, he would immediately say, "Stop talking to me like one of your employees."

This invalidation and manipulation eroded my confidence, stole my identity, and kept me silent. It's part of why my job was so important in keeping me alive. It was the place where my ideas were not only welcomed, but led to actual business results. People saw me there, they saw my worth, and my leadership potential. I was not required to be silent and small there.

I remember being really bothered by how Kevin treated his parents and how over the years we had distanced ourselves from my parents. It was like the acceptable attitude was that our parents were dysfunctional, less wise than us (or "him"), and were a nuisance. I remember mentioning to Kevin that I felt like God was speaking to me about honoring our parents. I told him that I remembered the scripture in Ephesians 6:2-3 that said honoring our father and mother was the first commandment with a promise attached, "so that it may go well with you, and that you may enjoy long life on the earth." I told him if we wanted it to be well with us and live long, that we needed to make some changes in how we treated our parents. Kevin was furious — he didn't want to be corrected. He blew off what I said and walked away.

It wasn't just big topics like honoring our parents where he told me I was wrong. When Kevin and I disagreed about a past event or memory, he would always say, "We all know your memory is bad." When we would have decorating choices in our home, he would frequently override my opinions and make the final decisions on furniture or art because "we know you don't really have an eye for these things." He made most of the decorating decisions. I went along with him because I didn't want to argue.

10 - He kicked me when I was down.

It seemed Kevin only agreed with me when it was a topic that made him bigger and me smaller, or something that made him right and me wrong. He seemed to revel in situations where I was humbled or corrected.

The most painful example of this was when I was chosen to participate in an executive coaching program at my job. This was an annual program where only a handful of high-potential vice presidents and senior vice presidents were to work with professional coaches to improve their leadership capabilities and self-awareness.

The process was to start with me selecting about ten people to give me feedback by way of a survey, and the executive coach specifically asked me to choose people I knew had an issue with me or would give me strong, or even harsh feedback. The goal was to identify any potential career blockers and to make some adjustments in my leadership style, so I could be more successful in the long-term.

A lot of the survey feedback I received was extremely positive. It reaffirmed many of my strongest leadership qualities and unique attributes: that I am great at solving complex problems, that my energy and enthusiasm inspire others to buy in, that my diverse skill set was an asset to the company. But as expected, there was also some feedback that was super hard to hear. The executive coach sat down with me to process and discuss it. Some of the feedback included things like, "Rebecca has a hard time listening to others when she's made up her mind," and "Sometimes with Rebecca, it's her way or the highway."

The coaching process did a really good job of helping me see myself from the perspective of others, so I could make some adjustments. Even though some of the feedback was difficult to face (and even made me cry), I look back on it as a critical time in my career because I was focused on how to be more self-aware and appreciate different styles.

Kevin and I had some friends over for dinner and I shared with them about this coaching experience. I told them a bit of the constructive survey feedback and how difficult it was to acknowledge.

I can still remember the pain in my heart when Kevin entered the conversation. "FINALLY someone told you the same thing I've been feeling all along. All this time you've acted a certain way and it's been really hard for me to deal with. I feel so vindicated now."

The reason this was so unfair (besides the fact that it was simply cruel), is that I wasn't strong, assertive, vocal, or opinionated at home. I was totally the opposite. At home, I had become a silent, compliant, obedient, and doting robot. Kevin was reveling in taking the opportunity to kick me when I was down. In his eyes, the smaller I became, the bigger he could be.

Being married to a person who revels in your frailties is abusive.

A SECRET, SILENT KILLER

Most people in my life never saw the realities of the emotional abuse I suffered in my relationship with Kevin, as it was extremely hidden. No one at work ever suspected anything was amiss at home. A few of those who were closest to me (as close as people could be, between my walled-off heart and Kevin's suffocating restrictions) did see some concerning things, but there were two reasons why for the most part, the emotional abuse was completely hidden.

The first reason the abuse was hidden is because I outwardly projected "everything's good, I'm happy, we're fine" at all times. While we were married, I always hoped Kevin would come to his senses, and change. I thought by acting as if we were a happy married couple, we would eventually become one. But more than that, I was still afraid of failing at my marriage and afraid of others believing something was wrong in our family. Like in my childhood, adolescence, high school and college days, and my experience with Henry, my core motivator was still to perform so I would not be rejected by others and by God. I simply could not entertain the thought of things not working out with Kevin. I had vowed to never divorce again, and the religious obligation I felt was a powerful force.

CHAPTER SIX: LIVING IN THE CURSE: EMOTIONAL ABUSE AND NARCISSISM

The second reason the abuse was secret was because above all, Kevin valued and treasured his image. He was extremely concerned about being seen and perceived as smart, successful, handsome, financially wealthy, and even as humble and Godly. In our house, everything revolved around making sure Kevin felt good about himself, so he wouldn't punish me with bad treatment. His focus on his image and preserving a positive impression on others at all costs motivated him to carefully navigate situations so as to never be judged poorly. Sometimes he would put on a grand show for others of our relationship and how great it was. Of course I would follow along, because I was scared of not agreeing with him and putting him in a foul mood.

Emotional abuse is a secret, silent killer. Unlike physical abuse, that can be seen, emotional abuse creates hidden wounds. These wounds may not create physical pain immediately, but they can inflict just as much, or even more, damage to individuals.

While someone remains in an active emotionally abusive situation, the wounds inflicted to the heart and soul of the victim never heal. They are constantly ripped open, getting infected, festering, and then getting ripped open again. The suffering party is often completely isolated and alone in their grief. I would strongly argue that healing from emotional abuse is never possible while one remains in an emotionally abusive situation.

Having a constantly hemorrhaging heart resulting from ongoing emotional and psychological abuse is arguably one of the most painful experiences a human can endure.

Are you the woman in my dream? Are you sitting in your living room, attending a Bible study pretending to be fine, while inwardly you are malnourished, bald, on life support, and about to drown? What's crazy, is that ever since I woke up from a life where I was secretly and silently dying from constant emotional abuse, I have suddenly begun to see how many women are in this situation, especially those in the church. And just like I was, they pretend to be okay, and might actually think they are okay, although they suffer from the deepest forms of human torment, manipulation, and control—stuck in shackles forged by the enemy. I believe millions of women live in secret, silent prisons of emotional abuse, with no one there to say, "Bring them back!" (See Isaiah 42:22). The curse from Genesis chapter three is alive and well in our world.

I AM THE HUMMINGBIRD

The first time I ever remember hearing the word "narcissist" was in the one (and only) professional counseling session I attended with my first husband, Henry. The counselor saw the signs in that meeting and was able to put words to the pain I experienced but didn't know how to express.

I don't enjoy using labels like "narcissist" or "introvert" or "extrovert" or "co-dependent" or anything else that has the potential to unfairly peg someone into a profile or personality type that overly generalizes or is somehow unfair. I also believe in the power of our words and declarations (especially as believers in Jesus) to bind and loose things (see Matthew 16:19)—to call things into being (on the positive side) or to focus on the bad and prevent good change from happening (on the negative side). I don't ever want my words or labels to create the potential to keep others in bondage. So I'm proceeding with caution here. It's not helpful to go around calling people names, and the momentary pleasure and satisfaction of declaring someone else is a narcissist is actually a trap (we will discuss the trap of the victim and self-justification later).

I'm also not a licensed psychologist or counselor, and I haven't deeply studied narcissistic personality disorder. However, I want women who have experienced emotional abuse at the hands of a narcissist to know they aren't alone, and they certainly aren't the first.

That said, here is my personal definition of a "narcissist." Narcissists are the most insecure people on Earth. The only thing holding them together—their source of strength—is the admiration, regard, and accolades of others, which create a sense of security and safety that they require to function. Therefore, the most important thing to them is their image and power. They also completely lack empathy, the ability to share or understand others' feelings. Narcissists do not have the ability to empathize with someone else, because they are so consumed with themselves and their image. This lethal combination of deep insecurity, hyper-focus on projecting an image of strength and greatness, the need for power to feed their self-image, and the inability to empathize with others is a perfect recipe for emotional abuse. Narcissists feed their need for power so skillfully that they always ensure they maintain a positive image to others, while wreaking havoc on the woman they control, without any regard or understanding of the damage they inflict. In my experience, narcissists aren't blameless, but they also aren't aware of the web of control, manipulation, and abuse they have woven around themselves in an effort to become powerful, and to be perceived by others and even themselves as the person they want to be.

It's interesting how those who have had intense personal experiences with a narcissist really understand their dynamic, but those who haven't, usually don't.

I believe the scripture God gave me in 2 Timothy 3 (the one that gave me the courage to end things with Mauricio, the warlock) actually talks about narcissists, and we should not be surprised that this kind of person who preys on weak-willed women is going to be common in the last days:

> *But you need to be aware that in the final days the culture of society will become extremely fierce. People will be self-centered lovers of themselves and obsessed with money. They will boast of great things as they strut around in their arrogant pride and mock all that is right. They will ignore their own families. They will be ungrateful and ungodly. They will become addicted to hateful and malicious slander. Slaves to their desires, they will be ferocious, belligerent haters of what is good and right. With brutal treachery, they will act without restraint, bigoted and wrapped in clouds of their conceit. They will find their delight in the pleasures of this world more than the pleasures of the loving God. They may pretend to have a respect for God, but in reality they want nothing to do with God's power. Stay away from people like these! For they are the ones who worm their way into the hearts of vulnerable women, spending the night with those who are captured by their lusts and steeped in sin. They are always learning but never discover the revelation-knowledge of truth (2 Timothy 3: 1-7, TPT).*

A few days after I "woke up" during my coffee date with Claire, I reached out to a friend named Jean to talk about things. To me, this was a risky move. Jean served as a mentor to Kevin as he was growing up, and I was terrified that someone like her, whom I trusted, who loved Jesus, and was close to the Holy Spirit, was going to tell me that I needed to stop this nonsense and just deal with Kevin and stay with him like a good Christian wife. But I felt strongly that I needed to speak to her, so I did.

When I first arrived at Jean's house, she was in her dining room fretting over a hummingbird who had flown into her house but couldn't find its way out. The hummingbird rammed into the wall and the ceiling, trying desperately to get free. Jean was trying to help it along with a broom carefully, but unsuccessfully. After several minutes, she decided to give up and try again later. We went to chat in another room.

I sat down with Jean on her couch and began to share what was going on with Kevin. About three minutes into my sharing she stopped me and said, "He's a narcissist." I burst into tears—relieved she wasn't going to judge me and correct me, but she actually understood. She knew immediately after what I shared. The reason she knew this is because she had encountered a few such individuals in her life.

I was starting to see that when it comes to narcissists, if you know, you know.

Because narcissists are deeply insecure, obsessed with their image, and unable to empathize, it makes them the primary perpetrators of emotional abuse in relationships. In fact, I suggest that emotional abuse and narcissism almost always go hand-in-hand.

Meeting with Jean that day was significant for me. God had begun to connect me with so many supportive people who understood my situation and were committed to walk with me and pray for me, wherever God was leading.

Before I left Jean's house, we went to check on the hummingbird in the dining room. It had eventually found its way outside to freedom. Her eyes filled with tears as she said, "Rebecca, you're the hummingbird."

CHAPTER SIX: LIVING IN THE CURSE: EMOTIONAL ABUSE AND NARCISSISM

CAN NARCISSISTS CHANGE?

When I first started learning about emotional abuse and narcissistic personality disorder, I did quite a bit of reading on whether or not narcissists can recover and under what conditions. Coming from a spiritual perspective, I wanted to know whether there were examples of narcissists getting set free from this tormenting darkness. I looked for any evidence that Kevin wouldn't always be this way. And to be honest, what I was able to find was extremely sparse. Some reputable studies show limited progress of behavioral change, but almost no documented cases of complete and sustained psychological turn-arounds.

But that doesn't mean it hasn't happened or it isn't possible. I believe God can do anything and can change any heart. My favorite example of this is the apostle Paul. He was Saul, who believed he was righteous and doing God a favor by supporting the persecution, arrest and murder of believers in Jesus. Acts chapter nine tells us that what finally got a hold of him was Jesus himself, calling out to him on the road to Damascus, "Saul, Saul, why are you persecuting me?" By the time Ananias was sent by God to pray for him, a transformation had happened in his heart, and he was not only healed of his blindness, but was filled with the Holy Spirit and was preaching about Jesus in the synagogues within the hour.

I do believe it's possible for narcissists to change. If Saul (Paul) could do a complete turn-around, then even the toughest narcissist can, too. But I also believe the scriptures that say God gives grace to the humble. There are dozens of scriptures that point out that God can only redeem a <u>repentant</u> heart. He does not force himself upon his people, He respects our free will.

The difficulty for the narcissist is whether they have the capacity, strength, or desire to humble themselves so God can come in and heal them. Admitting their frailty is the one thing they cannot do - because this would disrupt the very core of their operating system.

In a way it reminds me of the "unforgivable sin" which is grieving the Holy Spirit. It doesn't mean that God won't forgive us for grieving the Holy Spirit, but it means that when we grieve him, he doesn't have the ability to come in and move in our hearts and convict us of sin, to bring about repentance and restoration. The narcissist who cannot see or admit his depravity does not position himself to be redeemed and stays in perpetual darkness.

God resists the proud, but gives grace to the humble (James 4:6b, NKJV).

CHAPTER SIX: LIVING IN THE CURSE: EMOTIONAL ABUSE AND NARCISSISM

QUESTIONS FOR THE READER:

1. How are emotional abuse and narcissism outcomes from the fall and the curse in the garden?

2. In what ways has emotional abuse impacted your life or the life of someone you know?

3. In what ways is emotional abuse potentially more damaging than physical abuse?

4. If narcissism is going to be common in the last days according to 2 Timothy 3, can we expect that emotional abuse will also become more prevalent? How can God's people respond to this? How does Paul instruct us to deal with these people in this scripture?

5. How can a narcissist be healed?

READ THIS PRAYER OUT LOUD:

Jesus, thank you that you don't desire for me to live in any hidden places of bondage. Thank you for revealing anywhere that I've been living in abuse, where I've been used in a way that I was not designed for. I thank you, Jesus that you don't desire for me to suffer with heart pain forever, but you came to set the captives free and to heal every wound. Thank you for the light of your truth, and thank you that you are going to take my hand and lead me out of the darkness. Thank you for sending me people who know how to walk with me out of the prison I've been living in, partnering with the Holy Spirit (where there is liberty) and not partnering with a spirit of religious obligation. Jesus, thank you that you weren't motivated by adhering to the religious regulations of the Pharisees, but you were motivated by kindness, compassion, and the freedom for every captive who turned to you with an open heart. God, I believe you are able to rescue me, redeem me, take care of me, silence my fears, and heal my heart. I commit myself to you, and I trust you, in Jesus' name.

# Part II

Chapter Seven

REMOVING THE YOKE

Stand fast therefore in the liberty by which Christ has made us free, and do not be entangled again with a yoke of bondage.

Galatians 5:1 (NKJV)

IN THE HILLS

The day after I woke up, I went on my favorite walk up in the hills behind my house. I almost never saw other people on that trail, and I felt free to sing, cry, dance, and pray. For the few years leading up to my awakening, I would always pray the same way on these hill walks. I would ask God to restore joy to my life. I would ask him to use me to save the lost. I would ask him to forgive me for living selfishly and to forgive me for sometimes getting angry with my children. I would ask for more patience for Kevin and for God to show me how to love him. I would run out of things to pray, then I would pray in my prayer language, which I received many years before when I was filled with the Holy Spirit.

The more I would pray in the Spirit, the more I would feel bile rising in my throat. And if I kept praying in tongues I would sometimes start gagging. Now you remember this same thing happened when I closed the door to Mauricio and told the spirit of lust to leave. I knew I was in a spiritual battle, and I needed to get free from a certain darkness that had a hold on me, but my mind didn't connect this at all to what was going on with Kevin. Instead, I focused on what I was doing wrong in life. I asked God to change me, to refine me, and to help me be like him. I asked him to show me what I needed to be delivered from. I felt so far away from him. What happened to that person who was bold and powerful and free and prayed for CEOs on international business trips?

The few weeks leading up to when I woke up, around the same time I had the dream about the drowning woman, my hill walks started to change. I would hear God saying he was going to prune me. I heard him say I was going to walk through the valley and I needed to take his hand. I heard him say that he couldn't put new wine in an old wineskin. Finally, when I asked him why I wasn't walking in the fullness of his plan for me, I was reminded of the dynamics with my spouse. This was all very disorienting. I wanted to walk in fullness, but I didn't see Kevin changing, and it was going to be impossible to do it unless he was on board. I still lived in a lot of deception, but this part was clear: I was never going to be free to do all God had called me to do if I remained in the oppression I had been living in for nearly a decade.

On the day after I woke up, I had an entirely new perspective. I now realized while I was still far from perfect, that the strife in my life, the state of my heart, and all the pain I felt was mostly not self-inflicted, but mostly the direct result of Kevin's treatment.

Walking in the hills, I had no idea what to do next. I felt God urging me to call John, my dear friend Bev's husband. John had been a pastor on staff at our church at the same time as Kevin, and he was familiar with our situation.

John answered my call on the first ring. I could not have been more relieved to hear his voice on the other end of the phone.

I told him what happened, that I had woken up.

"Thank God," he said. "It's about time."

I was surprised, but also not surprised at his response. He and Bev had been waiting for me to decide I wasn't going to stay asleep anymore. They had seen firsthand the dynamics in our home and had tried many times to talk sense into me that Kevin's treatment was not acceptable.

His advice to me on the phone that day was really clear.

"You can't fix Kevin. Kevin will have to decide if he wants to address what's going on in his own heart. Let me say it again: you are not responsible for fixing him. Your job is to focus on fixing you. Here are the questions you must now answer: Why did you allow this? Why was it acceptable for you to live like this for so many years? Why didn't you say no? Your focus cannot be on fixing Kevin. He might lose everything, and he will have to make his own choices. But you must focus on YOU—figure out how you got here. And get to the root of it and get healed."

I could actually hear God through John's voice. The truth of what he said rang clear in my spirit. I was determined not to set my focus on fixing Kevin. Lord knows I had already tried that, for years, unsuccessfully. Now

I needed to focus on the one part of my life I was actually responsible for: fixing myself.

ISAIAH 58

I got home from my hill walk and my conversation with John with renewed resolve. I found Kevin in the office.

"We need to talk," I said.

"So talk," he said. He was grumpy about something going on at work.

"We need to talk about our marriage. I am not okay living like this. I refuse to believe this is what the rest of my life is going to look like. I am in so much pain from how you treat me. I feel like you treat me worse than most people treat their worst enemy."

He actually rolled his eyes. "Here we go again," he said.

Old habits die hard. After several attempts at getting through to him calmly, I got mad and raised my voice. I probably hurled a few insults and accusations. I told him for the hundredth time we needed couples counseling.

"You go to counseling if you need it," he said. "Seems like that would be a good idea for your anger issues."

I'm not sure how long we went round and round. Finally, I tried a different approach. "I'd like to go to the prayer service at the church up the street tonight. Do you want to come?"

"I'm not going to prayer," he said. "And you don't need to go either."

Now in our usual interactions, I might have negotiated or even begged to be able to get him to agree to let me leave that night. More likely, I would have just stayed home because the conflict wasn't worth it. But I couldn't. This was a defining moment.

"I'm going," I said. I made dinner for the kids, got their pajamas on, gave them big hugs and kisses, and left.

I wasn't regularly attending church, but I had gotten connected through my mom to a wonderful woman named Lori who was Spirit-filled. She had become really interested in supernatural healing because her husband had a traumatic brain injury. She had introduced me to a church up the street that held worship services similar to my old church: long and unstructured, and a lot of freedom. That night, they had opened up their building for people to come and independently pray and seek the Lord. It was perfect timing for me. I needed to get out of the oppressive environment of my house and into God's presence.

Once, many years before and during my "great awakening," I had a significant experience hearing God speak to me during a similar prayer service. So I had a lot of faith that God was going to meet me there that night. There is something about going somewhere with the expectation of hearing God that gives it permission to happen.

I found a place to sit, and then I found a place to lay. Fortunately, this wasn't the kind of church to frown upon laying down in prayer services, and I was glad for that. I asked the Holy Spirit to come, and I felt him immediately. It was a safe place to let down all my defenses. I couldn't hold back the floodgates of tears that came, and came, and kept coming. I let them come. I had held them back for so long. I wasn't sure the tears would ever stop, my well of pain was so deep.

For the very first time that night, I told the Lord about my pain. I told God about the agony I felt in my marriage to Kevin. I asked God why Kevin was like that. I told him I couldn't handle the shame of another divorce. I told him I didn't want to put my kids through hell. God already knows what's in our hearts, but there is something extremely important about our choice to let him into our honest places of pain. He always meets us there. His word says, before we even finish asking, he already sends help (see Isaiah 65:24).

Then I asked God to speak to me. I told him I would be brave and do whatever he told me to. I told him I trusted him and if he wanted me to stay married to Kevin I would do it. I asked for direction. And I heard him whisper to me.

"Isaiah 58," His whisper said.

I sat up and grabbed my Bible. I braced myself. I honestly thought God was going to tell me something about unconditional love or about forgiving seventy times seven times or about turning the other cheek. But as I read the chapter, a few things literally flew off the page. It was verse six that said:

CHAPTER SEVEN: REMOVING THE YOKE

"Is this not the fast that I have chosen: to loose the bonds of wickedness, to undo the heavy burdens, to let the oppressed go free, and that you break every yoke?" and verse eight that said, *"If you take away the yoke from your midst…then your light shall dawn in the darkness."*

God didn't throw religion at me that night. He didn't tell me to pipe down and submit to my husband and go back to sleep. He didn't tell me that "he hates divorce" or chastise me for being unhappy in my marriage. No, he told me very clearly to remove the yoke of oppression. And then I heard him whisper, "You will not walk through this alone."

FIRST BOUNDARIES

A few days later, after the kids had gone to bed, I had a serious talk with Kevin. I told him that I was not going to live like this anymore, and that I needed three things from him.

First, I needed him to sleep in the downstairs guest bedroom. I needed personal space. I suggested we not make a big deal out of this for the kids and just say that he was sleeping in a different room so we could both get better sleep.

Second, I needed him to work from somewhere else during the day. I could not focus on my job with him sitting in the same office. I asked if he could please go work at his mom's house or a coffee shop.

Third, I told Kevin I was not going to talk to him about our relationship without a counselor present. I explained I didn't feel safe discussing our marriage, my feelings, or my heart alone with him. I told him that I wasn't ready for any couples counseling because I had made appointments with a therapist and an inner healing counselor, and I wanted to try and sort out myself a bit first. I recommended he do the same.

Kevin agreed to my three requests. By this point, I think he realized I was serious about this, and I wasn't going to just stuff all these issues down again. For the first time, it wasn't going away.

I believe a man who was truly repentant, humbled, and willing to make radical changes would have behaved a certain way in this moment. He would have taken this opportunity to say something to make me believe he wanted to fight for me, to fight for our marriage—something that indicated that he wanted to get help, to really change—that he cared for me, and he would do his part, something to show he was willing to accept his role in our problems and take a humble path where God could come in and change him.

Instead, he said, "Can you please not tell anyone about this?"

His response disgusted me, but was so typical. There was not a hint of remorse in his voice, but only the obvious manifestation of his single deepest fear that his precious image would be tarnished when others found out we were having problems and that the perfect "power couple" wasn't so perfect after all. He didn't seem worried about the state of my decimated heart, nor willing to really take a good look at his own behavior, but unsurprisingly, he was most concerned about what others would think of him.

"No, I will not agree to keep this a secret. I'm done suffering alone," I said. I had no idea at the time how important this choice would be. The role of other people in my freedom process would be significant, and God had said that I would not walk through this season alone.

"Well, can I at least choose therapy or inner healing, but not do both?"

I couldn't believe this was actually what he chose to say to me. He was already negotiating the minimum amount of work he was required to do in order to "fix things."

"Do what you want," I said. "I'm going to work on myself."

THE TRAP OF THE VICTIM

Before we move on in the story, it's important to take a minute to touch upon a major (and super tempting) pitfall to avoid at this point—which is to focus entirely on the abuser's role in the failed relationship and to get stuck there.

In the case of me and Kevin, it was really important for me to realize, after almost ten years of denial, that while Kevin's behavior toward me was extremely wrong, abusive, and undoubtedly inspired by dark spiritual forces at work, it was still done through an act of his own free will. It was one hundred percent wrong and sinful. Freedom from emotional abuse requires us to recognize the abuse is wrong, and the abuser is very wrong for doing it. You can't get free if you don't first realize you've been in bondage.

However, my own patterns of dysfunction, unresolved people-pleasing tendencies, and my own free will choices to participate in the cycles of abuse were all contributors to our unsuccessful relationship. After waking up, there is a very strong temptation to fully allocate "blame" to the abusive, narcissistic party and to camp out there forever in a place of seemingly comfortable self-justification. But unfortunately, this is not the path to healing—it's the trap of the victim. It's a trap because you're so focused on what was done to you, that you don't focus on what you need to do to break the cycle.

Again, recognizing that you've been subjected to emotional abuse is an extremely important step in your freedom process that cannot be skipped. You will never have the courage to exit an abusive situation if you don't fully believe that you've been in one. But after that, only focusing on the sin and spiritual depravity of the other person isn't the way ahead. Like John told me, you must take a very big step forward and focus on your own freedom…it's a shift from external focus to internal focus. And I don't just mean freedom from the abusive situation itself, but freedom from the pattern that keeps repeating in your life (or the pattern that will continue repeating in your life until you address it at the root), freedom from the deep emotional wounds that now mar your heart, and freedom from shame, regret, and trauma.

For me, the step of walking out of a victim mindset and into freedom was significantly more difficult than the step of realizing I had been abused. All my pain had now come to the surface (after being stuffed away for years), and it was loud, ugly, and desiring vengeance. At this point, there was a huge temptation to take on a victim's identity. We've all met these people who live as a victim—they dwell in a place where the only thing feeding them is the reassurance that someone else was wrong and they were right. It feels good for a while, because it always feels good to be right, and to some extent, it feels good when others feel sorry for us. But it's false nourishment, and it quickly makes a person bitter and twisted. The false security of "he was wrong, and I am right" is a counterfeit form of healing.

If you find yourself "needing" to tell others how terrible your abuser was or if you feel like it's your duty to open the eyes of others to the evil he represents, you are probably stuck in an unhealthy place. Focusing on him isn't going to bring you to the other side. Keep walking. Don't get stuck in the victim's trap.

To avoid it, resist the urge to take on the identity of a victim. Instead, push forward, to the identity of an overcomer. An overcomer may have been victimized, but they refuse to allow that to define them. They refuse to make their life story about how someone wronged them. Instead, an overcomer takes the hand of Jesus in the dark place and lets him lead them out step by step, to the place where their life story isn't that they were abused, but that they've been made totally new by God.

Jesus paid to remove every curse, to heal every hurt, and to return us to our original place in the garden. An overcomer does not deny what happened to them or glaze over the gravity of the prison they lived in, but they take the hand of Jesus and walk out of that prison into freedom. If we take his hand, he will lead us until we are fully healed. But hear this: healing doesn't finish when the abusive situation stops. Healing <u>starts</u> then.

The fullness of healing is free, but it is not cheap. The freedom process is full of fears and uncertainty, like walking blind into the unknown. But his promises are sure. If you can trust him to lead you out of captivity, he will do it. He will not leave you or forsake you.

QUESTIONS FOR THE READER:

1. When you ask the Lord very honestly what things in your life are holding you back from walking in the fullness of all he has for you, what does he say?

2. What is a "yoke" and what does it mean for someone in an abusive situation to "remove the yoke of oppression" according to Isaiah chapter fifty-eight? What is the result of the yoke being removed, according to this chapter?

3. How can a person acknowledge they've been gravely abused, but become an overcomer instead of a victim? Can you identify places in your life where you may be stuck in the trap of the victim?

READ THIS PRAYER OUT LOUD:

Jesus, thank you that the veil separating us was torn from top to bottom when you paid for my freedom on the cross. I ask that you would show me every veil that still separates us, that you would give me eyes to see anything blocking me from stepping into the perfect plan you have for my life. Thank you that you did not design me to be abused or oppressed, but your word is full of your promises to set the captives free. Thank you for showing me how to remove every yoke of oppression. Thank you, Jesus, that your word says your yoke is easy and your burden is light. I lay aside now every yoke that is not yours, Jesus, and I accept your yoke. Thank you that you are kind and gentle, and that you trade my ashes for beauty. Thank you, Jesus, that you have called me an overcomer and not a victim. I lay aside now any identity of a victim, and its false comforts, and I declare that I will overcome, as Jesus also overcame. Thank you, God, that your Holy Spirit is with me, that I will not walk alone, and that you are going to bring me every person, support, and resource I need to exit my captivity and enter into freedom. I thank you that where the Spirit of the Lord is there is liberty, and that Jesus' greatest goal in coming to Earth was to free those who are oppressed.

Chapter Eight

STEPPING OUT OF THE CURSE

But the moment one turns to the Lord with an open heart, the veil is lifted and they see. Now the "Lord" I'm referring to is the Holy Spirit, and where he is Lord, there is freedom.

2 Corinthians 3:16 (TPT)

THE DEVIL IS A LIAR

When Jesus gave his life on the cross, he paid the full price to return us to our original state in the garden before the curse entered in. There is power in Jesus to restore everything that was lost and to remove every result of sin.

Stepping into the full inheritance of the cross looks like Genesis chapter one: men and women, both made perfectly in God's image, living in perfect intimacy with God and with each other, with shared dominion over the Earth. Now that Jesus has come, anything less than that reality is less than Jesus paid to give. I don't know about you, but I am going to keep pursuing that reality until I reach the end of my days. My greatest desire is to operate on Earth exactly the way God originally designed me to. All of creation waits for this (see Romans 8:19-21).

The devil comes to steal, kill, and destroy. His greatest desire is to keep us bound up in the curse and to keep us living in places of captivity, where we cannot and do not operate in the power, authority, and freedom that Jesus paid for. Even Jesus called him the father of lies (John 8:44).

Therefore, we should not be surprised the enemy uses very cunning and historically effective tactics to convince God's daughters to remain in places of oppression—places of the curse. In my story, there were five major lies the enemy tried to throw at me to keep me from entering into freedom. But for all five of these, God was faithful to reveal truth—to take my hand and to lead me out of captivity and out of the curse. It is for <u>freedom</u> that Christ set us free (Galatians 5:1).

LIE #1: GOD HATES DIVORCE

I don't think I would have been able to identify and overcome the barrage of lies the enemy threw at me in this season if God didn't send me several people with anointed, timely words of wisdom. One of these was Bev, the wife of John (whom I called the day after I woke up, and who encouraged me to not get stuck trying to fix Kevin, but to focus on fixing myself).

Bev is a wonderful, wise, beautiful woman. She was one of those who tried unsuccessfully to intervene and shed some light on what was going on during my marriage to Kevin. I had always known that her first husband had been cruel and abusive, but as she continued to share her story with me, what I learned was shocking. On their wedding night, it was like someone flipped a switch and he became someone else. He told her that she was ugly and it was hard for him to look at her. His cruelty surpassed that of Kevin.

Bev and her first husband had children together. She spent many years trying to love him, trying to be good enough, and praying for him to change. Meanwhile, he was known and respected in evangelical and spirit-filled Christian circles, traveling around the world with powerful speakers. He was a religious pretender, and almost everyone thought he was a great, spiritual, handsome guy. At home, he called his wife worthless and said he wished he'd never married her. Outwardly, they were a great couple. Secretly, he manipulated, controlled, and abused her to make himself powerful and important.

Bev stayed in years of emotional abuse because of the fear of "sinning by divorcing." She had grown up (like many Christians) to have a "no tolerance" policy for divorce and considered it to be off-limits. She was so tormented in her emotionally abusive marriage that she became extremely ill physically. There were days she could not get out of bed because of the pain she was in. She lived a hopeless life of captivity for many years. But like me, Bev eventually woke up.

A significant part of her freedom process was revelation regarding the scripture that reads in some translations, "God hates divorce." This scripture is probably the one every Christian calls to memory when asked, "What does God think about divorce?" It is probably also one of the scriptures most frequently and egregiously taken out of context. I believe the enemy has used this out-of-context scripture to keep millions of women captive for fear of doing what they believe God hates.

We find "God hates divorce" in some translations of the second half of Malachi chapter two. I highly recommend reading it and coming to your own conclusions about what God is saying in this context.

Malachi is the last book in the Old Testament. Before Jesus, God's people were operating under the Law of Moses, which is the first five books of the Bible (the "Torah"). Malachi, written by the prophet Malachi, is a message from God to Israel that primarily deals with corrections to bad behavior: priests offering defiled offerings, impure sacrifices, and cutting corners in serving God. God says, through his prophet, "You have departed from the way; you have caused many to stumble at the law" (chapter one verse eight).

Here is the section about divorce (Malachi 2:13-16, NKJV):

> *And this is the second thing you do: You cover the altar of the Lord with tears, with weeping and crying, so he does not regard the offering anymore, nor will he receive it with goodwill from your hands. Yet you say, "For what reason?" Because the Lord has been witness between you and the wife of your youth, with whom you have dealt treacherously; yet she is your companion, and your wife by covenant. But did He not make them one, having a remnant of the Spirit? And why one? He seeks Godly offspring. Therefore take heed to your spirit, and let none deal treacherously with the wife of his youth. "For the Lord God of Israel says that he hates divorce, for it covers one's garment with violence," says the Lord of hosts. "Therefore take heed to your spirit, that you do not deal treacherously."*

It's really unfortunate how out of context "God hates divorce" actually is. The primary focus of this passage is not about God hating divorce, it is about God rebuking men in Israel for treating their wives treacherously. In fact, their treachery is so vile toward their wives, that it covers their garments with violence (or in some translations, covers their garments with blood). This scripture makes it clear that what God actually despises is this treacherous behavior of men treating women improperly. In fact, he despises it so much, that he no longer regards their offerings and their outward religious activities, like covering God's altar with weeping and crying. He rejects their offerings, because of how poorly they treat their wives. Their sin against their wives is so offensive to the Lord, that he no longer hears their prayers, weeping, crying, and their offerings. He will not receive offerings from men who pretend to honor God but in the meantime treat their wives with treachery. Let me say it more bluntly: the Bible is clear that God will not hear or answer the prayers of men who abuse their wives.

Now read verse 16 of this same passage in the New International Version (which does not include the language "God hates divorce"):

> *"'The man who hates and divorces his wife,' says the Lord God of Israel, 'does violence to the one he should protect,' says the Lord Almighty. So be on your guard, and do not be unfaithful."*

Whether or not the original text should be translated as "God hates divorce" is potentially unclear. What is abundantly clear, however, is how God feels about men who treat their wives (the ones they "should protect") with violence and treachery. Proverbs 6:16-19 (NKJV) gives us a clear list of the six things God actually hates (notice that divorce isn't on this list):

> *"These six things the Lord hates, yes seven are an abomination to Him: A proud look, a lying tongue, hands that shed innocent blood, a heart that devises wicked plans, feet that are swift to running to evil, a false witness who speaks lies, and one who sows discord among brethren."*

This list really helps us understand the nature of God and what offends him to the point of hatred. He doesn't get offended by the lack of religious adherence to religious rules, but he is offended by pride, lying, hands that are violent to the innocent, wicked schemes, and feet that rush to evil. It's not the matter of "to divorce or not divorce" that is primary in Malachi chapter two, but the focus on the oppressive, abusive way men in Israel treated their wives. This must have been happening frequently enough that the prophet Malachi took the time to issue a written rebuke that ended up in the canon of scripture.

God isn't saying, "I'm angry at you for not upholding the religious rules." Instead, he says, "I do not acknowledge your religious activities because of the way you are oppressing those under your care."

Taking this a step further, let's look at the focus of Jesus. During his entire ministry on Earth, the people who hated Jesus the most, and ultimately crucified him, were the Pharisees who were so offended about Jesus breaking the religious rules— that they aligned with the spirit of the accuser of the brethren (e.g. the devil - Revelation 12:10) to kill him.

And what's so shocking is this: Jesus <u>did</u> break the religious rules! He healed the man with the withered hand and allowed his disciples to pick grain on the Sabbath, and he fraternized with tax collectors and sinners. But Jesus said the most radical and compelling thing in response to his religious accusers. He said in Matthew 9:13 (NKJV) one of my favorite Jesus quotes of all time: "Go and learn what this means: I desire mercy, not sacrifice."

When you think about Jesus' perspective, which values mercy over sacrifice, it's easy to prioritize freedom from oppression and abuse over religious adherence to rules and regulations. And it becomes easier to discern well-intended Christians who operate in the spirit of the Pharisees— the spirit of the accuser of the brethren. Know this: God never comes in accusation. We must learn to know the difference between the heart of Jesus and the heart of the Pharisees. Jesus called them a "brood of vipers" (Matthew 12:34).

The more I saw and understood God's nature, and his thoughts toward me and my situation, the more freedom I received from the lies that had entangled me.

LIE #2: YOU WILL MESS UP YOUR KIDS

The second greatest lie that kept me in captivity was the false belief that leaving my oppressive marriage was going to have a catastrophic impact on my children.

We all hear the negative statistics about the children of divorced parents ("kids from broken homes"), and I don't doubt these statistics are true for a broken world with broken people who operate in brokenness. But when Jesus enters, he makes all things new, and he is able to redeem and restore not only the women, but the children of broken relationships. He isn't going to redeem the woman but leave the children to the wolves. He is able to rescue everyone.

Consistent with what God had already started, I received wise counsel and heavenly wisdom in this season from the most unexpected places. Friends from college, whom I hadn't spoken to in years, were getting a nudge from the Holy Spirit to call and check on me and to share encouraging scriptures. I received a call from Susan, the mother of a dear friend from home. Susan and her daughter had pulled me aside when I was engaged to Kevin and unsuccessfully tried to talk some sense into me. She knew and understood what I was going through.

I will never forget what Susan said to me when we spoke. She spoke about my children. She said I would be tempted to believe I must stay married to Kevin for the sake of my children, because "kids of divorced parents always get screwed up." She presented a different perspective: that kids who grow up in a house observing an interaction between parents that is full of dysfunction, abuse, trauma, and strife, would get a lot more screwed up than if they divorced. She asked me if I wanted my two sons, whom I loved more than anything, to learn how to treat a woman by observing how their father treated me.

This hit me hard. I was terrified of screwing up my children and believed, because I had been conditioned to believe it, that divorcing was the worst thing I could ever do for my kids. The thought that they would be more damaged if I stayed married to Kevin was totally new. I imagined my kids observing Kevin's indifference toward me. I imagined them observing how I tiptoed around, catering to his every need, never expecting any kindness from him, and never receiving any. I imagined them forming an understanding of how to treat a woman by observing our relationship. I imagined them in their own adult marriages, treating their wives with the same cruel arrogance, selfish disdain, and sharp treatment because they grew up seeing their father treat their mother that way.

I am one hundred percent convinced that if I had stayed asleep and in captivity, managing my pain with alcohol, easily irritated, and unable to connect authentically with others, my kids would be in really bad shape because of my limited capacity for healthy parenting (in addition to the catastrophic dysfunction they would have observed in their parents). But, God!

I was grateful for advice like Susan's that was full of God's truth, although part of me wished someone would sit me down and tell me I needed to suck it up and figure out how to save my marriage. At least that would be my comfort zone: to endure pain and suffering by putting myself aside, and stay in bondage. Despite the pain, it was all I had known in my adult romantic relationships. But none of the people God sent me heaped religious duty on me. Neither did they give me advice to divorce Kevin. They simply were there—supportive and available with kindness, truth, and love that I didn't know I had needed all those years. Everyone somehow knew the choice was mine, and learning to make choices about my life and my future was key to my healing process.

LIE #3: IT'S BETTER IN EGYPT (YOU WON'T HAVE ENOUGH)

Unlike many women in abusive marriages, my situation was unique in that I had my own career and steady income. God had provided for me and my family through my job in significant ways, and I was grateful. It certainly helped me to not fear I wouldn't have enough money on my own (although I wouldn't fully break free of that fear until later in the story). I can understand how women must feel who want to leave captivity, but they remain because their role during the marriage was less about producing income and more about focusing on children and family.

I would never criticize a woman for making a choice to stay home and raise her kids, as long as that was the desire of her heart and what she felt called to (and wasn't coerced into staying home by a husband threatened by her being a powerful person outside of family life). I believe some of the most powerful people on Earth are the obedient, praying, stay-at-home-moms who have captured the heart of the Lord. I am absolutely sure that some of these do more for God's kingdom than the most famous Christians with big public platforms; and some of us are going to be surprised when we get to Heaven at the eternal reward some of these praying moms will receive, who weren't known on Earth at all—but are well known in Heaven.

One of the greatest lies the enemy leverages to keep women in captivity is that they must remain, because they must rely on their abusive partner for finances, because otherwise they would not have enough to live. The fear of not having enough is one of the most powerful, deceptive motivators. In fact, it was so pervasive in Jesus' day, that he addressed it directly in the Sermon on the Mount. He said,

> *This is why I tell you to never be worried about your life, for all that you need will be provided, such as food, water, clothing - everything your body needs. Isn't there more to your life than a meal? Isn't your body more than clothing? Look at all the birds - do you think they worry about their existence? They don't plant or reap or store up food, yet your heavenly Father provides them each with food. Aren't you much more valuable to your Father than they? So, which one of you by worrying could add anything to your life? And why would you worry about your clothing? Look at the beautiful flowers of the field. They don't work or toil, and not even Solomon in all his splendor was robed in beauty more than one of these. So if God has clothed the meadow with hay, which is here for such a short time and then dried up and burned, won't he provide for you the clothes you need - even though you live with such little faith? So then, forsake your worries! Why would you say, 'What will we eat?' or 'What will we drink?' or 'What will we wear?' For that is what the unbelievers chase after. Doesn't your heavenly father already know the things your bodies require? So above all, constantly chase after the realm of God's Kingdom and the righteousness that proceeds from him. Then all these less important things will be given to you abundantly (Matthew 6:25-33, TPT).*

CHAPTER EIGHT: STEPPING OUT OF THE CURSE

Does anyone actually believe it is possible to put seeking God's kingdom first while living in the enemy's captivity? I think it's impossible to step into your kingdom purpose while living in shackles. Jesus said, if we throw off all that hinders and seek his kingdom first, everything else will be added. He will provide for all our needs, according to his riches in glory (Philippians 4:19). Everything on the Earth is his (Job 41:11), and he owns the cattle on a thousand hills (Psalm 50:10).

I know, it's scary. But believing that another human (or even a job) must financially provide for you to meet your needs is actually idolatry. I can't tell you how many times after I divorced Kevin that I asked the Lord to send me a Godly husband who had a great income to reduce the pressure on me financially. Every single time I prayed this carnal prayer, I heard God's swift rebuke—he immediately reminded me that <u>he alone</u> is my provider, and any other mindset is deception. I'm so grateful God corrects those he loves (Hebrews 12:6). Believe this: God <u>will</u> provide for you.

When the Israelites were delivered from slavery in Egypt, they were afraid. They had to run through the miraculously parted Red Sea to avoid being killed by Pharaoh's army. They left behind the comforts of their daily routines, their homes, and a predictable pattern of life. Sure, life in Egypt was full of torment and oppression, but at least they knew what to expect. They had cried out for freedom for four hundred years, and God was faithful to deliver them from the hand of their abusers. But walking out of a slavery situation into freedom can be scary. There are no predictable patterns or comfort zones, only major uncertainty. Many times, they grumbled and complained to Moses and even said, "It would have been better to stay in Egypt."

Once God parts your Red Sea and you walk across and out of captivity, it's natural that you will feel scared, uncomfortable, disoriented, and might even long to return to the comfort of your former enslaved situation (a bit of "Stockholm Syndrome"). At least back there, things were predictable. Tortuous, but predictable. Can you imagine if the Israelites actually returned to slavery in Egypt because of fear of the unknown in the wilderness? You can't go backwards…only forward. The road to freedom is a new road, full of new experiences, and can only be traveled with the help of Jesus. Take his hand. The Lord is with you.

If your story is anything like mine, you may have a pattern of returning to Egypt that has repeated itself in your life. What I've come to understand through counseling and with the help of the Holy Spirit is that I was subconsciously avoiding men who were kind and doting, because I didn't have any emotional structures for that. Kindness from men was terrifying. The kind of relationships that "felt like home" to me were cold, and then I could do what I always did—perform to try to earn their love, affection, and kindness.

Choosing to step out of captivity is going to be full of unknowns, new ways of thinking, and new ways of God providing. Don't be surprised when it seems a bit disorienting and outside your comfort zone. This is what getting a new wineskin feels like! But don't partner with fear, and don't long for the false security of Egypt. Remember what Moses said, "For the Egyptians whom you see today, you shall see again no more forever. The Lord will fight for you, and you shall hold your peace."

LIE #4: YOU ARE A DUCK

The devil twists scripture to keep us in captivity. He's been around a long time, and he knows the Bible better than we do. Some of the biggest lies that keep women in bondage are the voice of the enemy that whispers, "Shouldn't you just turn the other cheek? Doesn't love always protect, always trust, always hope? If he takes your coat, you're supposed to give him your shirt, too." The enemy tries to convince us that God wants us to stay, because if we were Godly enough, we wouldn't be wounded by the emotional abuse, but "real Christians" would rise above it…letting the water roll off our backs like a duck. The voice of condemnation speaks shame, guilt, and obligation, and it blames us for the results of others' mistreatment.

Reminder: God's voice never comes in condemnation. Nor does God use scripture to keep his children in captivity. His plan and heart for us is freedom. It's why Jesus came to Earth! He desires mercy, not sacrifice.

I was still believing some lies. A big part of me still was ashamed that I wasn't a "duck that let the water roll off its back" in my marriage with

CHAPTER EIGHT: STEPPING OUT OF THE CURSE

Kevin. I hadn't been strong enough to not be affected by him. His words and behaviors did wound me, deeply. I wondered if someone truly stable in God would have been stronger, better.

Judy (who introduced me to the concept of emotional abuse) invited me to join her at a church about an hour away. She had signed us up to receive a prophetic word during their weekly prayer night. I didn't know this church, and I'm sometimes skeptical about getting a word from strangers in a church I'm not familiar with, but I also knew it was up to me to test the word, and whether to accept it. One thing I did know: God's Spirit was alive and well on Earth, and prophecy is part of his plan to strengthen, encourage, and comfort His people (1 Corinthians 14:3). I had a lot of faith that God was going to speak to me.

When it was my turn, a man and a woman sat down with me and invited the Holy Spirit to come. They waited on the Lord for a while, which I thought was a good sign. They were asking him for his heart for me.

The word I received that night was a significant and surprising one: that I was a delicate flower. I had been in some strong wind and some really rough conditions, with turmoil hitting me from the left and from the right, and the flower had taken a bit of a beating. But I was God's own very delicate flower—I was made that way. Some people didn't understand I was a delicate flower, so I had been bruised and damaged emotionally. God knew I had been through a lot. He was going to cover me, protect me, heal me, and let me release my pain to him. He had captured every one of my tears. He has always been there with me, even in the tough times, and I'm his beautiful, delicate flower.

This word had me weeping. It swept away all the self-criticism and accusation about not being stronger and more spiritual and not being more immune to the wounds I had received. It reminded me that I was made as a delicate treasure, not designed to be squashed or bruised. It gave me permission to want to be tender again. It wasn't weakness, it was tenderness. Not hunkered down and hiding, but open-hearted and blooming.

Several weeks later I was at a birthday party when I was talking to a woman about a particular situation she faced. She had a friend for years who was terrible to her. The friend was manipulative, controlling, cruel, vindictive, and abusive.

It's funny how sometimes you give someone advice and it feels like an out-of-body experience where you're really talking to yourself—and giving yourself advice.

This woman said, "I know I should be stronger. I should be like a duck, letting these mean things she says roll like water off my back. I'm trying to turn the other cheek."

All my righteous indignation rose up in that moment. I felt the power of the Holy Spirit as I said, "No, you are not a duck. You should not just stay there, being abused, and feeling some sense of obligation to stay and take it and try to let it roll off your back. You're not a duck! You're a delicate flower! God didn't make you a duck - he made you a flower. You were never meant to endure that kind of treatment from another person."

I think we were both shocked but the truth resounded in our ears. "You are totally right," she said. "Wow." But I had also convinced myself I was no longer going to believe the lie that I needed to be stronger, more resilient, and try harder to deflect abuse. I was stepping out of the lie and into the truth that I was actually a delicate flower, never made for abuse.

LIE #5: YOU DON'T HAVE A CHOICE

I hadn't seen my friend, Annie, since she visited Kevin and me during our first year of marriage. She was there during my great awakening, when I received my first prophecy about Psalm 51 that blew my socks off, and she was there the night I heard angels singing. But after her visit, when I confronted Kevin and he blamed her for causing trouble in our relationship, I wasn't able to maintain a connection with her. Kevin did not approve of me interacting with her.

I reconnected with Annie when I woke up. It was like we hadn't missed any time together. She had started her own prophetic ministry and her own personal coaching business. She was one of the most tremendously gifted, wise, and anointed people I had ever met. She booked a trip to visit me with three other ladies from her ministry team. I could not wait to see her! I was grateful she still wanted to be friends after all these years of me dropping off the Earth. God was continuing to send me the people I needed to encourage and strengthen me in this season.

Annie asked if we wanted to schedule a night of prophecy and invite a few people who we knew needed to hear from the Lord. It was a night to remember. Annie and her spiritual daughter, Amy, prophesied to every single person in the room—not fluffy, short prophecies, but life-altering, powerful, words of destiny and hope.

I was the last one to receive a word. We had been there for several hours, and I had been crying the whole time. Nothing is better than witnessing the raw power of the Holy Spirit to bring a fresh word of life to God's people, especially those who had never experienced God's gift of prophecy before. There wasn't a dry eye in the place. It had been a long time since I had been in a prophetic ministry setting.

Since Annie knew what was going on in my life, she let Amy prophesy over me. She purposefully didn't tell her anything about my personal situation, because she wanted the word to be pure and unclouded. All Amy knew was that I was in a tough spot and I needed some direction from the Lord.

Amy prophesied over me for more than ten minutes. It was significant, and about the Lord re-pouring the foundation of my house—a foundation with no cracks, holes, or faults. I was extremely encouraged. But then, Amy texted me the next morning to tell me the rest of the prophecy she didn't want to release publicly because it was more private and personal.

She said, *"I saw the entire picture of the Lord re-pouring the foundation of your house, and hanging off to the side of your house was a huge solid block of ice. And in that solid block of ice was your husband frozen. He was not moving or looking, he was just frozen. And I heard the Lord say, it was your choice to thaw him out or leave him be - that it was up to you to get him in the process or not. But the important part was that the thawing process is a long process because he was in so much ice! You could do it if you wanted, but the Lord was giving you permission to choose."*

In my heart, I had hoped God would speak to me with a booming voice from the sky, saying, "It's time to divorce Kevin." And maybe that actually happens to some people. But part of the destructive pattern in my life that needed to be addressed was blindly following the choices of others to please them, instead of using my own. And God had clearly said, it was up to me to choose. If he had chosen for me, the destructive pattern would have continued. I would have deferred to someone else's choice, and the "people pleasing," conforming, complying, and adhering to the decisions of others would have been perpetuated. I understand now that the cycle of people-pleasing cannot be broken until one starts a new pattern of decision making, that is focused on making decisions based on what I need, not what everyone else needs.

God wasn't manipulating me. He wasn't saying "You can choose, but only one answer is right, and one is wrong, and you better pick the right one." God isn't a manipulator. God wanted to pull me out of the lie that I had no choices, and show me that I had always had all my choices. He gave them to me in the garden, and he gives them to me still.

I already knew what I wanted to choose. I wanted out of this torture chamber called my marriage. But I remembered the disdain in the voices of Christians when they talk about others and say judgmental things like "they've been divorced twice" or "they're on their third marriage." I remembered some Christian friends coming over to talk to me when Henry and I filed for divorce, looking me in the face and saying "divorce is a sin," and that was their entire message to me: "you're sinning." I remembered my pastor encouraging me to include in my wedding vows that I would never "consider" divorce, because divorce was "not an option."

None of my hesitations about divorce were because I thought Kevin was going to change and be restored or because I thought God actually wanted me to stick it out with him for another decade or two. In fact, every revelation I had received from the Lord in this season was about removing the yoke of bondage and stepping into freedom from captivity. No, all of my hesitations felt like they were coated in a slimy package of shame, judgment, and religious obligation. I was worried about what some people would think of me. I was scared of their hurtful accusations. The spirit of religion is mean, and it can be very wounding.

There's a reason Jesus stands at the door and knocks. He's not barging in, but offering to come in. Scripture, from the very beginning of time, is full of God giving his children choices. Love in relationships can only exist where choice exists. The most powerful thing he has ever given us was our choices. When we use our choices to enter freedom and leave behind religion, power is released. When we choose mercy over sacrifice, we align with the heart of Jesus.

I CHOSE FREEDOM

Kevin and I had set up a first appointment with a licensed psychologist and marriage and family therapist named Dr. Bacon, and it happened to be the day after Amy gave me the word about God giving me permission to choose. Kevin and I had spoken to two different counselors on the phone, and we both agreed on Dr. Bacon. She was a Christian, and had many years of experience with situations like ours. We had both spent a little time with her on the phone explaining our perspectives.

We sat down in Dr. Bacon's office, and she cut right to the chase.

"Your old marriage is over. I think you can both agree on that. Now it's up to you to decide where to go from here. Do you want to make a six-month commitment to trying to build a brand new marriage together, or, have you decided that you do not want to build a new marriage together, and it's time to part ways?"

This was kind-of a shocking way to start. I think the two of us expected the Christian counselor to give us a spiel about God restoring our relationship. I'm so glad she didn't. She knew from speaking to us that we didn't really have a marriage to restore.

Kevin piped right up saying he was committed, that he didn't want to get divorced.

I sat there looking at the man I had married. I believed him, that he didn't want to get divorced. But I knew it had nothing to do with having any care or concern for me, and everything to do with protecting his image. He didn't want to be perceived as the guy whose wife divorced him. Especially if people knew why. I knew his image meant more than anything to him, and divorce would devastate it.

Dr. Bacon and Kevin waited for my response to the question. I was scared out of my mind. I silently asked God to help me.

I will never forget that moment when the presence of God filled Dr. Bacon's office. I felt warmth like a fire start to spread up my arms, from my wrists to my shoulders. "Be strong," He seemed to whisper. This was perhaps the most terrifying moment of my life. I could already hear the voice of religious condemnation coming at me: "You didn't try hard enough," "You didn't give him enough time," "You should have turned the other cheek," "You are damaged goods."

But I could recognize the voice of the accuser. The voice of God never comes in condemnation. My arms burned with the presence of the Holy Spirit. "Be strong, be strong, be strong," he seemed to say.

I gathered all of my courage, and said, "I am done with this marriage."

"Why?" asked Kevin, shocked.

I explained the best I could. I said my heart had been completely annihilated by him. I said he treated me worse than most people would treat their worst enemies. I said I was utterly alone, and after years and years of trying to communicate my pain to him, of telling him I didn't want to have sex with someone my heart was not connected to, of asking if we could get help, I was finished. Nothing I said was new. He had heard me say these things for years.

He argued with my explanation. He didn't agree with my assessment. He didn't remember all the times I had confronted him. He said this was the first time he was hearing it. He acted surprised that I was so wounded.

I explained again. This time, I told him that when I read my "husband list" all those years ago in Africa, and he said that it perfectly described him, that I realized now it wasn't true. I had just blindly believed him. Almost nothing on my list was actually true about Kevin. I had almost broken up with him after reading the people pleaser book only to get talked out of it by Kevin and someone who gave me really bad counsel.

He rolled his eyes when I brought up my husband list. He argued again. He asked for a better explanation.

I explained again. This time I used the words "emotional abuse" which seemed to make him extremely angry. I gave several examples. He started to argue with me again when Dr. Bacon stopped him.

CHAPTER EIGHT: STEPPING OUT OF THE CURSE

"Kevin, I think she's explained enough. It's clear what she's decided. What will be important for you now is to focus on yourself and understand how you got here."

I think Kevin was embarrassed. I'm sure he was expecting the Christian counselor to try to talk me out of the decision that I had made, but she hadn't. Instead, she stopped me from having to explain myself a fourth and fifth time and had redirected Kevin towards self-examination and his own path forward.

Dr. Bacon pivoted the discussion to divorce mediation. She wanted to give us some tools for next steps. She highly recommended we jointly choose a mediator to help us agree on the terms of our split, rather than each of us choosing expensive attorneys that could drag us and our children through a combative, lengthy, and expensive court process. She offered a few mediator references for us and cited some research regarding how this path could be lower conflict and therefore less difficult for the kids.

I regretted riding in Kevin's car to see Dr. Bacon. We didn't speak on the drive home. I was about to enter the most difficult season of my life. But freedom was coming, because I had chosen freedom. God was with me.

QUESTIONS FOR THE READER:

1. If you were the devil, and your greatest priority was to keep women from stepping into their original design, what strategies would you use most often to keep them captive?

2. What does it mean when Jesus says, "I desire mercy, not sacrifice?"

3. Which of the five lies the enemy tells women to keep them in oppression and bondage have you experienced in your life or observed in the life of others?

4. What are the areas of your life where you've believed that you or others are the ones who must provide financially, when God wants you to step into the truth that he is our provider?

5. Are there places in your life where you've believed you don't have choices because of religious obligation, but God wants to show you that you've had all your choices all along?

READ THIS PRAYER OUT LOUD:

Jesus, thank you that your word says when we turn to you with an open heart, every veil of deception keeping us apart is removed. I open my heart to you now, and I ask you to search me and show me any veils you want to remove. Thank you that the Spirit of God brings freedom, and that you are freeing me from every lie. I ask that you would give me the mind of Christ, and that your Holy Spirit would speak to me in the still small voice, in my dreams, through the Bible, and through people you send me who are filled with your wisdom. Thank you that you didn't leave me to walk through this season alone, but you are with me, and you send others to walk with me as well. Thank you for giving me discernment when a spirit of religious obligation tries to attack me, and for freeing me from the religious strongholds that once motivated my actions and behaviors. I declare over myself that

CHAPTER EIGHT: STEPPING OUT OF THE CURSE

whom the Son sets free is free indeed, and that your plans for me are good, to prosper and not harm me, and to give me a future and a hope. Thank you that you are giving me hope instead of despair, that you are leading me out of the winter and into the spring. Thank you for giving me a new wineskin for a new season, and give me grace, because the new season feels different. Thank you that none of my pain will be wasted, because what the enemy meant for harm, you meant for good.

Chapter Nine

FREE INDEED

Therefore behold, I will allure her, will bring her into the wilderness, and speak comfort to her. I will give her vineyards from there, and the Valley of Achor as a door of hope; she shall sing there, as in the days of her youth, as in the day when she came up from the land of Egypt. And it shall be in that day, says the Lord, that you will call Me "My Husband" and no longer call Me "My Master," for I will take from her mouth the names of the Baals, and they shall be remembered by their name no more.

Hosea 2: 14-17 (NKJV)

THE TRAP OF SELF-JUSTIFICATION

The morning after I told Kevin I wanted a divorce, I threw up…a lot. Some people don't barf when they get delivered from demonic oppression, and you can certainly get set free without barfing (I know many people who do). Sometimes it's as simple as revoking the permission you've given to darkness and agreeing with God's word. The enemy can only oppress you where you give him permission to do it. But I knew that morning because of my declared choice to exit my oppressive marriage, I had broken agreement with the demonic stronghold of religious obligation that had held me paralyzed for nearly a decade. Now I was free of it. I wasn't free of Kevin, because our battles are not with flesh and blood, but free of the forces of hell that kept me enslaved.

That morning, I might have been delivered from major darkness, but I was still very scared. I felt like the Israelites leaving Egypt. They may have been free from generations of torture and slavery, but at least there was some stability and predictability in Egypt. Now I had zero control and zero idea what was ahead. This was not at all comfortable for me. What would happen with our children? How would I be able to live without them in a shared custody situation? Would we have to sell our house, split the proceeds, and buy smaller, separate homes? As the party with a higher income, was I going to have to pay him child support and alimony payments? The path ahead was not going to be fun.

And just because I had experienced some big freedom, didn't mean the enemy wasn't going to now throw everything including the kitchen sink at me—to accuse me and condemn me for breaking the religious rules. It's important in this situation to remember Jesus never comes in condemnation and that Jesus always values freedom of captives over religious adherence to the law. He always desires mercy over sacrifice. The sacrifice he desires is an open heart, not performance. I was reminded and anchored by the Psalm of David that was given to me during my great awakening, in my first ever prophetic word:

> *For the source of your pleasure is not in my performance or the sacrifices I might offer to you. The fountain of your pleasure is found in the sacrifice of my shattered heart before you (Psalm 51:16-17, TPT).*

That said, I have to tell you that the religious accusation of well-intended Christians when I decided to get divorced (both times) was one hundred percent the most agonizing thing I've ever experienced in my life. Maybe it's because the religious spirit of the accuser of the brethren is the same murderous spirit that crucified Jesus. I'm telling you, <u>nothing</u> hurts more.

I was not surprised when Kevin told everyone who would listen that I had really lost it, that I refused to commit to six months of couples counseling, and that I had gone off the deep end and asked for a divorce. I understand why this was his approach. It was the only path forward for him that somewhat protected his image and portrayed him as being a victim rather than the opposite. I'm sure he even believed this story. In this season, I was deeply wounded by a few betrayals. My greatest fear—that I would be judged and condemned by Christians—definitely materialized.

Claire, who had woken me up, had spent some time one-on-one with Kevin after we met with Dr. Bacon. I am not sure what exactly he told her, but when I next spoke to her on the phone, it was like she had forgotten our conversation when she woke me up. She also seemed to have forgotten a dream she had where she found Kevin and me in prison cells, and while I let her take a key that said "by His stripes we are healed" and remove my shackles, Kevin refused to come out of the shadows and be freed. Her voice on the phone sounded different, and full of empathy for Kevin's plight. She said to me, "I'm not sure about the decisions you are making, I really think you need to slow down." After thinking for a few moments about what was happening, I said, "I love you, but I'm not sure I can be friends with you if you plan to remain close to Kevin." I knew this kind of triangulation of religious accusation would only create pain for me. I could recognize the voice of the accuser. I was not going to invite the enemy into my inner circle, and Claire and I didn't connect again after that. I mourned her friendship.

Some friends back home who were in our wedding party, texted me saying they wanted to talk. They had spoken to Kevin and wanted to make sure I was okay. Before I picked up the phone to call them, I asked God for wisdom. And he told me clearly that I was not supposed to explain my divorce decision or defend myself to them. It was obvious right away they were fully on board with Kevin's story. It was extremely hard not to give them my full defense, but I didn't, because God asked me not to. They didn't seem to be looking for my perspective, either. I said goodbye, knowing that it was the end of our friendship. I felt really betrayed. And it was hard to let them keep believing the story Kevin told them. Who else would he tell, and how far would the lies spread about me? But I knew attempting to keep friends who were also friends with Kevin would have been an open door for the enemy to continue to accuse and condemn me. All the access points needed to be closed.

I had become tentative friends with someone named May who had kids in the same preschool. We would get together sometimes to let our kids play together at a park. I didn't have many close friends, but she was close enough to have observed and asked me about Kevin's poor treatment. After our meeting with Dr. Bacon, Kevin called May to confide in her. He spoke to her (extensively, so it seemed), before I did about my decision to divorce Kevin. She texted me and said she was "praying for my marriage to be restored" and that "she was speaking to Kevin on the phone several times a day, "to make sure he was okay." Even though we weren't super close, this hurt a lot. She had chosen his side. It was too late for me to even share my perspective with her, she had been so thoroughly convinced that he was a victim and that I needed to stay married. Her betrayal was a painful one.

The major temptation at this point was for me to take up a defensive position and explain to everyone why I was divorcing, so they would not judge me. The inclination of my flesh was to openly reveal the horrid truths of how Kevin treated me in an attempt to smother their religious judgment using my own counter-accusations and the cold hard facts about how he had abused me for years. But this is another major trap, and it is not the path to freedom. If you defend yourself at the start of your divorce, you're still going to be doing it twenty years later. Self-justification is not a fruit of the Spirit. Jesus alone justifies us. God is our defender.

What you must avoid in the trap of self-justification is becoming an accuser yourself. If you feel the need to disparage the abuser to others, it is a good indicator that you're operating in self-justification instead of believing you have been justified by Jesus. More importantly, if you are surrounded by people who require you to explain yourself and your choices, or people who criticize your choices using shame or religious fear, you may consider whether these are the people God wants you to surround yourself with in your new season. Ask yourself if you have people in your circle who act like the Pharisees who condemned Jesus for choosing liberation over rules and regulations. Never forget: this murderous spirit of religion actually killed Jesus.

If God never comes to us in condemnation, we should remove the voices of condemnation from having access to us. This is an important part of forming healthy boundaries. I realize that most people who came to me with cautions and warnings about divorcing and prayers for my marriage "to be restored" were well intended, but also extremely naive. At this point, I was overwhelmingly sure that God's will for me was not for my marriage to be "restored." In fact, it was becoming clear that I never really had a "marriage" in the way God intended, I had been a captive the whole time. Only religion would try to push me back into a covenant with a person that tortured me for the sake of rule-following. That would certainly follow the curse, but not God's design.

I believe there are many well-intended Christian leaders who lack context regarding abusive situations, and who inadvertently encourage women to remain captives. I have been to many church services where someone prays and declares that God is going to restore all the broken marriages and stop divorce from happening. And every time, I feel a deep sense of mourning because these declarations assume that it's God's will for all people to stay married. In these situations, I look around the room to all the women I know who have left or are trying to leave abusive situations, and I can see how religious duty and shame are being piled on them. Jesus desires mercy, not sacrifice. He desires freedom over religious obligation.

I'm going to go out on a limb and suggest that divorce itself isn't the problem, but the brokenness between men and women that leads there. Divorce might be the visible "tip of the iceberg" sticking out of the water, but it's certainly not the massive body of ice underneath. Divorce is an outcome, not a cause - and it's the cause that needs to be addressed. Brokenness between men and women is a result of the fall, and the curse, and only Jesus can restore what was lost. It's a wonder every marriage without the power of Jesus doesn't end in failure. If we want to return to the garden, we don't start on the surface of things by trying to reduce the number of divorces—we go below the tip of the iceberg to address the pride, religion, and brokenness that sin brought into the world. Let's pray for the roots of pride and religion to be brought to light and healed. A lasting solution will tackle the cause (the curse) and not the symptom (divorce).

Don't misinterpret this as a universal endorsement of divorce. Of course if both parties of a dysfunctional marriage are humbled and repentant, and they want to stay married and aren't just living in religious duty, I'm all for restoration, and God can do it. But we must not value "the institution" of marriage over issues regarding freedom and captivity. Jesus didn't come to Earth declaring "I'm here to make sure no one gets divorced." He said, "I have come to free every captive." And I would suggest that abusive marriages where men rule over women have been a top form of captivity since the garden.

PEOPLE PLEASER NO MORE

When we come to him, sometimes God heals our dysfunction instantly. But sometimes he has to walk us through a process, like unwinding a ball of yarn. For me, I had been living in recurring cycles of people pleasing my entire life, and it was going to look like the "ball-of-yarn process" to get to the bottom of it. Beware of the allure of instant healing for decades of heart pain…it usually doesn't work that way. But I was determined to address it once and for all, and to end the cycle that kept repeating.

I got into therapy right away. Troy was a connection of Phil and Judy, and apparently had impressive credentials helping people who had been in abusive, narcissistic situations.

I will never forget the question Troy asked me in my first therapy appointment. He said, "Who told you that you need to comply?"

I can still feel the raw power of this question. It was <u>the</u> question. It was just like him asking, "Who told you to be a people pleaser?" Or phrased in a more spiritual way, it would have been like him asking me, "Where did you get this pervasive 'fear of man'?"

There's nothing like getting straight to the point. I knew exactly what he was asking. He was asking what was the root cause of my continuous cycle of believing that I needed to please, perform, and comply and not object, protest, or create boundaries in my life. At this moment, I knew I was picking back up the process I had started with Donna the counselor after my first divorce. We hadn't finished the process of addressing my people pleasing because I got short circuited by Kevin's emotional reaction and some bad counsel regarding my so-called "idol of independence." People pleasing forms a vicious cycle, because to break out of it, you end up disappointing people, and your core motivation is to not disappoint anyone.

Troy was not a Christian, and while I believed he could help me, I also knew I needed counsel inspired by the Holy Spirit. I asked my friend Annie, who was a prophet but also had a coaching practice, if she would take me on as a client in addition to my therapy with Troy

In my first session with her, she encouraged me that stepping out of people pleasing was going to look a lot like making new choices—every day—that weren't people pleasing. She gave me a homework assignment: every time I felt obligated to do something for someone else, to stop and ask myself, "why am I doing this?" And if it's any reason other than "I want to," then my answer should be no. It seemed simple enough.

I had no idea how difficult this assignment would be for me. I discovered that I was people pleasing all the time, doing things like hanging out with people I didn't particularly care to—solely because I didn't want to disappoint them.

If the homework wasn't difficult enough, I started having recurring dreams with a shockingly similar theme. I knew that when dreams repeated, you could probably count on it being God trying to show you something super important. Across the period of about a year, I had at least eight dreams with exactly the same scenario. In these dreams, I found myself in a compromising physical or sexual situation with a man (or woman) and I didn't want to be there, but I stayed because <u>they</u> wanted me to. God was showing me that the roots of people pleasing were still there. I needed to make different choices—choices not to stay in unhealthy situations to appease others, but choices to do what I wanted and what was healthy for me. Going back to the garden looks like stepping back into the place of having all our choices, and not relinquishing them to others.

In seasons like the one I was in, drawing near to the Lord was easy. I was so desperate for him, his peace, his voice, and his power to free me that I heard him all the time. I had been hearing him speak to me in the middle of the night, during times of prayer and worship, and through others. My journals during this time were packed full of heavenly revelation.

I had been seeing Troy the therapist twice a week for months. We had made some helpful progress looking at patterns in my life and mindsets that got me there. But something was wrong. Every time I brought up something significant God said to me, Troy redirected the conversation to what he wanted to discuss instead. Because he was not a believer, we were not incorporating the help of the Holy Spirit at all, and to me that felt like I was wasting time. I think you could continue in counseling or therapy forever without God directing things. But if you follow the leading of the Holy Spirit, what could take decades in traditional counseling can really be expedited.

In our first session, Troy told me that he was a narcissist. And the way he positioned it was that narcissists can become aware of their behavior and change to a certain extent, but the tendencies toward narcissism were more enduring. It was kind of shocking, but I thought maybe this would help him understand my situation better. In our first session, Troy asked me to promise that I would not exit the therapy process with him until we finished. He said that he's seen patterns before of women giving up before they were finished. And I did promise him, because he was the expert.

What I didn't know is that when I made that promise, I was relinquishing my choice. And just like that, I was back to deferring my choices to a narcissist to whom I had given access and authority in my life.

Hopefully this was the last time I would learn this lesson. I knew I wanted out of therapy with him. And I knew I was in trouble because I was completely terrified to tell Troy that I wasn't going to see him for therapy anymore. Not only would I be disappointing him, but more egregiously, I would be breaking my promise. I wanted to be a woman of my word. But promises made that attach us to any kind of control or manipulation are not to be kept. I knew I needed to discontinue with Troy and tell him in person that I was going to pursue counseling more aligned with my spiritual beliefs. Despite my great fear, when I went to his office and closed the door to him, it felt like I was telling every narcissist in my past "no." God was giving me opportunities to exit my patterns of people pleasing by making different choices. It didn't feel good to disappoint him—in fact, it was extremely scary. But this was an enormous step forward for me. I had recognized that I had been snagged again into a controlling situation where I had given away my choices, but I self-corrected and got back on track!

Just as Annie told me, stepping out of people-pleasing looks like making different choices every day. This was another opportunity to avoid the trap of the victim. Instead of thinking, "Why do all these controlling narcissists keep finding me—will this ever stop happening?" I decided to believe that God himself was putting me in situations where I could learn to be an overcomer. What the enemy means for harm, God means for good.

THE DARK NIGHT OF THE SOUL

Kevin and I scheduled meetings with two different divorce mediators so we could pick the one we liked best. One was recommended by Dr. Bacon, and the other by the therapist Kevin had started seeing.

The first mediator (recommended by Dr. Bacon) was a fiery woman with really strong experience and a strong personality. The second mediator (recommended by Kevin's therapist) was sweet, more passive, and more matronly.

I certainly preferred option one, while Kevin preferred option two. I wondered if it had anything to do with whom he thought he could more successfully influence into taking his side. I wasn't sure this was the battle I wanted to fight, and I was worried that Kevin would refuse to mediate (and instead get an attorney) if I didn't agree, so I went along with mediator number two: Sharon.

As the primary breadwinner in our family, I knew I was going to end up having to pay Kevin. Not just lump-sum money to split our savings and assets, but payments on a monthly basis for child support and probably also alimony. I had done some research about legal precedents in California, and I had a feeling it was going to be really painful for me financially.

In our first mediation session with Sharon, we talked about potential custody schedules. We discussed listing the house for sale and having photos taken to get ready for that. We also discussed our official "date of separation," which is used by the courts to calculate the length of the marriage and therefore apply standards for alimony or spousal support payments. Based on our date of separation, Kevin and I had officially been married for nine years and six months. Sharon explained there was a different precedent for marriages ten years or longer, and in some cases, this could result in "lifetime" spousal support payments.

Not surprisingly, Kevin tried to make arguments that our marriage should be "rounded up" to ten years, but Sharon held firm on the legal rules here. I realized—with no lack of extreme gratitude to the Lord for giving me courage and strength in that meeting with Dr. Bacon—that if I had agreed to a "six month process" of couples counseling, that our marriage would have met the ten-year mark, and the financial outcomes for me in the divorce would have likely been significantly worse. God's supernatural intervention and timing here were significant. He knew exactly when I needed to wake up, exactly what date I needed to tell Kevin I wanted a divorce, and when I would need him to help me make the right choices that would work together for my good. I was so grateful that "lifetime spousal support" was officially off the table.

In mediation meetings with Sharon, Kevin really turned up the charm. He projected all the things Sharon came to believe he was: a victim that wanted to stay married, a poor soul who was really surprised and shocked when I wanted to end it, a great dad, and someone who was easy to get along with. Overall, she was definitely neutral, as mediators must be, but her sincere empathy for him and his plight was sickening. How many more people would let him pull the wool over their eyes? Like so many, she saw the sheep's clothes, but not the wolf underneath.

As negotiations seemed to continue endlessly, I became more and more aware of the realities of my impending financial situation. I believed God would take care of me, but as time passed, it felt like I was losing more and more money to Kevin's demands, and I grew more and more worried about how I was going to make ends meet in my new reality.

When an executive recruiter reached out to me about a potential job, I didn't think much of it at first. But after a few conversations with the recruiter, I started to get pretty excited. This new opportunity was at a great, stable, public global company with a lot of possibilities.

The skills and experience required for this new role were a strong match for my experience, which was a pretty unique set of qualifications. I met with the recruiter several times, then I met with the executive who was hiring. Everything was going great. I had eight interviews and had completed a full capabilities assessment before the final interview with the president. By then, I had to repeat my credentials and qualifications so many times, it had really bolstered my self-esteem. It wasn't pride, but it was the truth about my skills, experience, and everything I could bring to the table. I was going through an important process that required me to say how valuable I was over and over again.

Meanwhile, the salary expectations I gave to the recruiter were aligned with the budget for the role, and my hope was rising. This was going to be great—I would get a new job with better pay just when I needed it—God had it all figured out! I believed this new job was God working out everything for my good. I needn't have worried about money.

The president had a big ego. During our interview, he talked about himself the whole time. I am not sure how he planned to evaluate my fit for the role when he gave me very little opportunity to speak at all. At the end, he said, "The entire team likes you so this interview is just a formality." I found it kind of awkward, but positive nonetheless.

When this company finally made me an offer, the recruiter was pretty disappointed. It was less than I was worth, and he knew it. The recruiter, who stood to make no money at all unless they hired me, encouraged me to decline the offer. He said, "The president doesn't think you are worth more than this. And if you accept this low offer, they will never respect you."

I was extremely conflicted, but this was one of those moments where I heard the voice of the Lord speaking to me through someone else. Was I going to take a job with less pay than I was worth, and go to a place where everyone knew I had accepted a low-ball offer? I declined the job, and I knew it was the right thing to do. It felt good for once in my life not to concede when it was related to matters of my own value.

But I was completely devastated. Now there was no solution on the horizon for my financial situation. I was getting plundered by Kevin, who was supported by a mediator who was supposed to be neutral but seemed to empathize with his every whining request, and he refused to move out until we agreed on everything, and his dark, brooding, hostile presence was around me twenty-four seven.

One night, I sat in my prayer chair in total, hopeless despair. I remember saying out loud, "God, are you even there? Do you even care?" It was my lowest moment. I felt there was no hope, no future. I felt like my agony would last forever. I even briefly longed for the security of my life in Egypt…I may have been asleep then, but at least I was not aware of all this pain.

But something happened to me that night in my prayer chair. I felt the Holy Spirit whispering to me. And suddenly I knew I would never have a moment like this again: a moment to trust God, against all odds. I would never have an opportunity to offer him this great sacrifice—the sacrifice of my trust, even when trusting him was the most impossible thing to do. I began to see this moment as the opportunity of a lifetime, to trust him when it would never be harder. I would never be able to make this sacrifice again. So I seized the moment and told him out loud that I trusted him. I told him I believed that no matter what it looked like right now, he was working all things together for my good. I told him that I believed his promises, and that I would not turn from him now. I only had one plan, and that was for him to work it out. There was no plan B. Sorrow may last through the night, but joy comes in the morning (see Psalm 30:5).

GOD'S MATH

I had been attending Jean's church and letting my kids sit with me in adult service with their electronic devices (even with the fear of being judged as "that" mother) because they really disliked the kids' class. I didn't want my kids to dread church. It was good for me to be in an environment with worship and good teaching, but I really could not see myself plugging in there. On Easter Sunday, no one got saved in the service I was in. It was then that I decided I still hadn't found my church. I was looking for a place where people encountered Jesus every week and where people worshiped like God was still alive, somewhere where the gifts of the Holy Spirit were still active.

My friend Lori suggested I try Oceans Church. It was really new and still small (meeting in a high school auditorium), but she had attended a conference there where a lot of people had significant encounters with the Lord (including her).

Our first visit, my kids connected immediately with the leaders of the children's ministry. To my amazement, they got checked in and waved goodbye to me. This was the first time they'd gone to a church kid's class without either major tears or major bribes or both.

The worship was really good. People actually worshiped more than performing. I sang at the top of my lungs. And the teaching was super dynamic, spirit-breathed. I took a ton of notes. I felt God's presence. I cried.

A few weeks later, I attended the informational class hosted by the senior pastor after the service to learn more about their vision and beliefs. When no one else had questions, I asked several, including their viewpoints on women in ministry and their views on building the kingdom versus building their own church. I really liked what I heard.

CHAPTER NINE: FREE INDEED

The next week, I brought Phil and Judy with me, as they had also been looking for a church. We sat together in the very back row. At the end of the service, the pastor (who had only met me once in the informational meeting) called me out by name and gave me a significant prophetic word. He said God was going to have me move in all seven spheres of influence. He said he saw me looking at my own resume, noticing places where I thought I had gaps, and a hand came and wrote the word "Jesus" in every place I thought there was a gap. I was shocked and really touched. I loved that prophecy was alive in this place. He also prophesied that the church would be known by its powerful women.

I asked the senior pastors if they would be willing to meet me for lunch. If I'm being really honest, I wanted to make sure they weren't going to take a religious position and judge me for divorcing. After all the freedom I had received, I was still afraid of religious condemnation. It was a touchy subject, and I didn't want to put myself in a position where the enemy had access to accuse me.

They didn't judge at all. They asked me if Kevin was a believer, and I said I honestly didn't know. They were kind, open, and loving. I knew that a church under their leadership would be a safe place to heal. I was so relieved.

I also knew God was speaking to me about giving. He said, "It's time to start tithing." It wasn't a "Now, now, time for you to be a good girl and follow the religious rules and give to the church." It was really different, more like, "If you trust me and live generously now, when you have the greatest fear of not having enough, watch and see what I will do for you."

I always know when God is nudging me on something. It doesn't feel like religion or condemnation, but an invitation into greater levels of trust, understanding, and freedom.

I already knew I was going to have to make monthly payments to Kevin, so this made it a terrible time by the world's standards to start giving ten percent of my earnings to God. None of my calculations had room for a tithe, even the calculations where I sold my house and moved somewhere smaller with a smaller mortgage payment, and figured out how to live with some major quality of life adjustments.

But God was relentless on this topic. I kept running across stories in the Bible where God's math didn't work like human math. I started a list of examples in my journal of "God's math:" the story of the loaves and fishes (Matthew 15), the woman who poured out the alabaster jar for Jesus (Matthew 26), the story of Elijah and the widow and the flour and oil not running out (1 Kings 17), the story in 2 Kings 6 of Elisha's servant's eyes being opened to see the heavenly army—that "those who are with us are more than those who are with them," and Jesus turning water to wine (John 2).

One Sunday, my pastor taught about the only scripture in the Bible that encourages us to "test God." God tells us to test him related to tithing, that we will be rewarded with abundance as a result for giving God his portion of our income. God says, "'Bring all the tithes into the storehouse, that there may be food in my house, and try me now in this,' says the Lord of hosts, 'If I will not open for you the windows of heaven and pour out for you such blessing that there will not be room enough to receive it'" (Malachi 3:10, NKJV).

The next Sunday at church I decided I was going to take the plunge and be obedient. While I was terrified of not having enough money to live on, I decided I was going to trust him. I began tithing that Sunday and never stopped. I decided to partner in that moment with my faith instead of my fear, and I had no idea how important that decision would be for my future. Every month after that, I had more than enough. My faith and obedience opened the way for God to take care of me in supernatural ways.

We had professional photos taken of our house so we could list it for sale. I was devastated about losing my house. After fifteen years of career advancement, using my income and bonuses to make smart real estate choices, and purchasing my dream home in California (which was my fourth home), it was going to be a serious disappointment to sell it. This house was everything I dreamed of, in a neighborhood I adored with walking trails and hills overlooking the ocean behind it in the distance. It had been such a gift from God to move here, and now I had to significantly downgrade.

It was the day before we planned to list the house for sale and hold an open house. I was folding the kids' laundry and listening to my recorded prophetic word from Amy when it hit me like a ton of bricks. Why hadn't I realized it earlier? I kept replaying this portion of the word:

> *"The Lord showed me a re-pouring of foundation in your life. It's like you've had your dream home, and you've lived in your dream home, but people would say, you have to knock down the home because you need a new foundation. And it's caused a fear because it's been your dream house - everything perfectly in place, every dream fulfilled. And you're asking the Lord, why would I ever throw away the dream and promise you gave me? And people would say, you have to throw the house away to replace the foundation. But I see the Lord intervening in such a unique way - where he lifted your dream home, and he re-poured a foundation like never before. It wasn't concrete, it was a substance of Heaven that was immovable, unshakeable, not one man, not one attack of the enemy could come against it. And the Lord so graciously held in his hand your dream home, and he gently laid it right on top of the new foundation he had placed, and he said, "I didn't want you to knock it down or give up." And the Lord held the integrity of your home together. I see the peaceful moment of you tucking your boys into bed. And the Lord said, "I have it - I have it tucked into place," and not to worry in the transition of the season of rebuilding of foundation, but to be at peace."*

I suddenly realized this word was not only symbolic of God restoring my spiritual foundation, but also about my literal house. He didn't want me to give it away—it was the fulfillment of dreams and promises, and I was to keep it. He was giving me a new foundation here. It was one of those moments where I knew beyond all doubt that God was saying I should keep my house and that he was going to work out the details.

And the math and the numbers did not work at all, but I knew God had spoken and he would make a way. I knew my children would be far better during the transition if we remained here—with their bedrooms, and our bedtime routines, neighborhood, and peaceful place.

Annie called saying she had a dream about me. In the dream, I stood in my house, and I said to her, "I kept my house." In her dream, I had re-decorated it in the way I liked, and my older son talked about how much he liked it. There were tornadoes swirling around me, but they didn't disturb me. I knew this was a confirmation. If God said it, I believed it, even though I had no idea how it would happen. I simply could not afford it. But God's math is not our math.

Three months later, I got a big promotion at work. It was totally unexpected, but I should not have been surprised at God's faithfulness. I had decided to trust him and be obedient against all odds, and he did not let me down. I was going to have enough money for my needs and to keep my house, just as he had promised. God is good indeed.

DIVORCED, BUT STILL IN BONDAGE

I sat at my piano and invited the Holy Spirit to come. I was preparing for another mediation session with Kevin and Sharon, and I was at the end of my rope. I wanted to be done, and I wanted to get out of this treacherous season and into the next. It had been more than four months of this endless process.

As I prayed, I asked God to come and show me anything I was doing that was keeping me from getting through mediation with Kevin. I asked him to remove any ungodly veil that was clouding my vision, keeping me from moving forward.

In a classic moment that I felt was constantly repeating itself in my life, as I prayed for God to free me from anything holding me back, I started gagging. I had to run to the trash can and vomit. As I've said before, not everyone barfs when they get delivered from darkness, but in some ways I'm glad that happens to me because it gives me the understanding (and faith) to know when freedom was taking place.

I asked the Lord, "What did I just get delivered from?"

And I heard him reply clear as day, "The belief that Kevin is one hundred percent bad."

Ouch. This one stung. As always, I knew it was God, especially because it wasn't anything I could or would have cooked up on my own. This line of thinking was not on my radar at all.

CHAPTER NINE: FREE INDEED

I realized that I did believe Kevin was one hundred percent bad. It was easier than believing God made him with a plan and purpose, and that there was good in him—the good that God put in him—and he was not fully and completely bad. There were no doubt forces warring within him, fears, bondages, trauma, and sadness. He was a captive of a different kind than me, but a captive no less, and one of God's children, as we all are. God loves each one. Kevin could decide to turn and repent and be fully restored, and God would wash away all his mistakes just like he had washed away mine.

I repented. It was hard. I confessed out loud that Kevin was not all bad. I asked God to remove any barriers or blockages holding back closure. I asked him to renew a right spirit in me. I asked God to show me how to forgive. I renounced the scary lie I had been believing that if Kevin humbled himself and repented someday that I would have to re-marry him. God does not punish us like that. If Kevin repented, it did not have the ability to harm me. If anything, it would be great for our children to have a father who walked in righteousness and not darkness. Kevin's freedom was his own choice, and it didn't have any ability to harm me. God was not asking me to stay married or obligating me to stay attached to Kevin in any way, but he was asking me to see Kevin as he made him.

That same day in mediation, after a long, painful road, we closed every issue. I didn't like many of the outcomes, but I knew the limits of Kevin's willingness to concede. We agreed on a full 50/50 custody, and we agreed on all the various payments I was to make to him. We agreed when he would move out, and which furniture he would take. It was finally over.

None of the things I relinquished to Kevin were surprising, but they were still big losses for me. But after all this time I had finally reached the end of the process, and I was relieved. Sharon prepared the paperwork, and we would both sign and file it with the court. We would finally be divorced, and he would finally move his things out. I could finally start my new life, life without Kevin's control. Or so I thought.

I realized quickly just how many of my previous life decisions had been deferred to Kevin. Most of my choices had been based on pleasing him or not disappointing him. It was almost like I had to learn to think for myself again.

When he moved out "his half" of our furniture, I felt a moment of sheer panic. How was I supposed to choose new furniture? I was used to always deferring to Kevin's choices. So I adventured into the unknown: I went to every furniture store in a thirty-mile radius and asked myself, "What do I like?" I didn't enjoy it at first. It felt like a lot of pressure. But I had lost my voice and my choices, and I needed to take them back. So little by little, I refurnished my house with pieces I liked, with art that spoke to me, with colors that calmed me. When I was done, I was extremely proud of myself. My house was such a gift, a real treasure. And I had decorated it how I wanted, and it felt like home—full of peace, hope, and safety. A haven. My kids and I were happy and secure there, just like God said we would be. We filled all our rooms with worship, and the peace of God permeated every space.

Perhaps even more disconcerting was when I realized I could dress however I wanted without constant fear of being criticized. This was big news for me. What did I want to wear? I asked my new friend Tami from church to go shopping with me, and instead of her picking things out, she helped me pick what I liked. I started to develop my own sense of style that wasn't designed to make me small or unnoticed. I bought rompers and jumpsuits, some sequins and velvet, and high-waisted pants and combat boots. I loved it all. And I celebrated the freedom I now had. It should have been this way all along. I was allowed to be creative and beautiful in how I dressed, and no one had access to tear me down.

In the early days after we finalized the divorce, I actually thought Kevin and I would learn to have a cordial relationship in support of our boys. All the co-parenting books talked about parents who could partner together and operate with trust and respect for one another, and I had hoped that Kevin and I would get there. But I quickly learned he was still the same person, and his need to control me didn't end when the divorce was finalized. Any time I didn't agree to his demands, I faced his full wrath. I suppose my need to please him and to do anything to avoid his hostility didn't end with the divorce, either. I was still terrified of his bad treatment. It was very easy to get triggered by him.

Any time I had a work trip upcoming, I would face overwhelming dread. I would gather my resolve, and reach out to Kevin: asking if he could take the kids when I was going to miss custodial time. He was not gracious. Sometimes he would ignore my messages and leave me hanging with no response for days or even weeks.

The agony I felt telling Kevin I had to travel when we were married continued into the divorce. The dread, fear, and anxiety were the same, maybe worse. The vicious cycle continued. Wasn't the point of getting divorced to get out of the controlling and manipulative environment? I had no idea how I was going to live with these dynamics until the boys grew up. Could I never escape this man's control and manipulation?

It was a year-and-a-half after the divorce was final. After six months of emailing back and forth with Kevin regarding the specifics of the upcoming New Year's custody schedule, I finally sat down with an attorney. I was looking for help.

The problem was: I agreed to all kinds of clauses in divorce mediation that said "parties will meet and confer" or where "consent is required." And while some co-parenting situations might have successful models for "meet and confer" or for requiring "consent," that was not the case here. I was kicking myself for agreeing to all these loopholes in mediation.

I was not surprised or shocked, but Kevin wanted to debate, negotiate, and ultimately "win" any time there was an issue that required us to "meet and confer." At least half the time, we ended up pulling in Sharon the mediator to help broker the discussion. The other half of the time, I agreed to what Kevin wanted because I didn't have the energy to fight him. It felt like we might be stuck in this same pattern forever.

I wish I had the foresight to know, a year-and-a-half prior when we were agreeing to the co-parenting plan that ended up in our divorce order, that meeting and conferring with Kevin was not going to be an ideal situation. Any interaction with him became an opportunity for him to assume his ever-present victim persona, to pressure me into agreeing with his point of view, to lament about how he was the only parent trying to work together, and to claim I was not being collaborative. I think he actually meant I was not agreeing to all his demands.

After a decade of almost always agreeing to Kevin's demands while we were together, it was hard to hold my ground. Where it was reasonable, I was flexible in compromising. But in areas that weren't equitable and I drew a boundary, nothing made Kevin more angry. This also wasn't surprising. The need he still had, that he most wanted, was to control me by getting me to agree to what he wanted, or to control me by getting me tangled into an emotional discussion where I lost my cool or hurled insults back. When I refused to take the bait and remained totally calm and focused on facts, he got even angrier.

MY DECLARATION OF INDEPENDENCE

I sat down with Sam the attorney to figure out my options. I couldn't imagine continuing on this path for twelve years until both kids reach adulthood.

"If there's things in your divorce order that aren't working for you, why don't you change them?" Sam asked. "It sounds to me like you are still married to this guy."

"You mean, take him to court?" I asked. I was already getting anxious about how furious Kevin would be if I went down this path, and how he would tell his family and everyone who would listen that I decided to stop collaborating using a mediator and involve attorneys. At this point, I recognized I was still concerned about what others would think of me because of his disparagement. But more than that, I was afraid of his angry response. I was still afraid of him. The thought of his ire directed toward me was terrifying.

Sam the attorney said, "I think Kevin has made it abundantly clear your generosity and diplomacy are not going to be reciprocated. Thus, you should probably either stop being so agreeable or stop complaining about him not returning the favor. I know this is harsh, but I think Kevin is the type that will continue to take without return, just like in your marital relationship. This is most likely why it is so irksome for you to have to deal with him, he continues to regress to the marital relationship, and you, not so much. I don't know him, but I think you've achieved a lot by way of mediation, perhaps more than could have been expected. However, expecting mediation to continue successfully may be a misplaced hope. I could be wrong, and if I'm misreading the situation, please excuse me. But it seems like every time you return to clarify the agreement, he comes away with yet another advantage or advancement of the connection while you are, from a big picture perspective, trying to sever the dependence. In other words, I don't think your agendas are in concert. Perhaps ask him if he wants to continue to have these battles and skirmishes or if he would rather learn to start to put the control button down? This might be a choice you need to make for him."

Ugh, I was not expecting Sam to say that. But he was right. It felt like I was still married to Kevin. All the levers of control and manipulation were still in full swing, and the marital dynamic of conflict still existed. It was time to really "divorce myself" from this situation.

The next Sunday morning after the worship service at church, a woman sitting behind me tapped me on the shoulder. I knew of her because she was part of a group of really amazing prophetic women in the area.

She asked if she could share a word with me, and I agreed. She said, "I see God removing two hooks from your back: the hook of manipulation and the hook of control. He is freeing you! And do you have sons? Because I hear the Lord say, he is giving your sons new DNA. I see that God has kept all your tears in a bowl. He is going to restore all the years that the locusts have eaten."

What an encouraging word. It was interesting the hooks she saw (that God was removing) were manipulation and control. I knew I was still being manipulated and controlled by Kevin. I could feel that I was still tied to his wants, needs, and demands. The image of these two hooks in my back said it all. But God was freeing me, and I needed to finish this process to remove the places where he still had access to manipulate and control me.

I set up a last mediation appointment with Kevin and Sharon. I was determined to make some big changes to our divorce agreement—to solve every open-ended, consent-requiring clause that kept me in a pattern of always having to return to him for permission and giving him constant access to torment me.

I prepared well for the session and sent an agenda of topics to cover. Unsurprisingly, Kevin didn't agree to a single thing. It was an awful, hostile conversation. He believed I would never get an attorney and address this, but he was wrong.

Sam the attorney was happy to hear that I had decided to use my choices to pursue changes to the agreements I had made in mediation and establish some real boundaries with Kevin. He asked me to sit down and write my declaration—a document filed with the courts explaining what changes I wanted to make and why. He encouraged me to write it as if I was reading it before a judge.

I have seldom felt fear like I did sitting down to write that declaration. I was completely bound up in terror about how Kevin would respond. I imagined his angry, hateful, disdainful, scornful response to me filing with the courts, and it was almost enough to convince me not to do it at all. Avoiding the pain and fear of his wrath was an old pattern that needed to be broken.

I needed to make my choice, and make my voice heard. I sat down and wrote my declaration, even though I was still afraid. I wrote that I chose to divorce because of the emotional abuse I experienced married to Kevin. I wrote that after a year of operating under the current agreement, that the constant conflict, need to meet and confer, and frequent involvement of the mediator was not a healthy situation for anyone including the kids, and my goal was to stop this cycle of conflict by addressing the open-ended issues in the agreement.

In that moment when I faced my fear of his hostile reaction, and wrote that document, the fear lost all its power. It would still be many months until I officially filed with the courts, until Kevin and his attorney responded, and until we had a court hearing with a judge, but all the fear of Kevin was now gone. It no longer had sway over me.

I was so relieved that I had been brave and pursued what was right for me and my boys, that I wasn't even worried about how the judge would rule. I knew I had done my part, and the rest was in God's hands. But the judge was wholly supportive of changes that reduced ongoing conflict, and she ruled in my favor on every issue of importance. It was finally over…I was finally free, for real this time.

QUESTIONS FOR THE READER:

1. Where in your life have you stumbled into the trap of self-justification? Are you still living in any places of self-justification, where God may be having a hard time defending you, because you are defending yourself?

2. Are there people in your inner circle who are voices of condemnation to you? Does the enemy have access to accuse you through anyone you've given an access point to torment you? What is keeping you from closing these doors?

3. Are there places of fear in your life where you are living in the world's math, but God might be inviting you to a greater level of trust, faith, and "his math?"

4. Are you stuck in a demonic stronghold of belief that your abuser is a hundred percent bad? Do you think this mindset is helping you heal and find freedom, or entrenching you more deeply in bitterness and anger?

5. What places of control and manipulation are you living in where you need to face your greatest fears and declare independence?

READ THIS PRAYER OUT LOUD:

Jesus, without you, I can do nothing. Thank you that you are near, that you love me, you are with me, and you will never abandon me. Thank you for giving me wisdom and discernment to see places I have been living in self-justification. Right now, I lay down my need to be right, to show others that I am right, and use counter-accusation to defend myself. Instead, I declare that God alone is my defender, and he will fight for me. I lay down my weapons now, and I align with Psalm ninety-one that I am safe under the shadow of your wing. I ask that any deception regarding others being one hundred percent bad would be removed from me now, and I ask for a heavenly perspective, even for those who abused and tormented me. God I thank you that it doesn't mean they weren't wrong to hurt me, but it does mean that I refuse to partner with the enemy to keep them enslaved in their captivity. I ask now, Holy Spirit, that you would show me any places in my life where there are hooks of manipulation still attached to me. I thank you, Jesus, that you paid the full price to free me from every snare of the enemy. Thank you for the people you have sent me and are sending me to walk with me. Thank you for the grace and strength to disconnect from people who aren't walking with me into freedom. I declare that God makes all things new, and he is making me new now.

Chapter Ten

CHRISTIAN FEMINISM

Then God said: "Let us make a man and a woman in our image to be like us. Let them reign over the fish of the sea, the birds of the air, the livestock, over the creatures that creep along the ground and over the wild animals." So God created man and woman and shaped them with his image inside them. In his own beautiful image, he created his masterpiece. Yes, male and female he created them. And God blessed them in his love, saying: "Reproduce and be fruitful! Populate the earth and subdue it! Reign over the fish of the sea, the birds of the air, and every creature that lives on earth."

Genesis 1: 26-28 (TPT)

JESUS WAS THE ORIGINAL FEMINIST

Either God made men and women as equals, or he didn't.

It reminds me of what C.S. Lewis said about Jesus in *Mere Christianity:* he's either the Son of God, as he claims to be, or he's a madman. We can't really have it both ways.

When we read Genesis chapter one and see that both man and woman were made in the image of God, and were both given rulership and authority to subdue the Earth, it's clear the design was equality.

The only reason the word "feminism" (the belief in the equality of women and men) exists at all is because Adam and Eve, through their sin and the curse in Genesis chapter three, put the entire history of the world on a path of gender inequality. Remember the spoken curse, which said, "Your desire will be for your husband, and he will rule over you."

I believe the word "feminism" can be such a negative trigger word in the church because it's been associated with a lot of things that aren't Godly. But this is no different from "Christianity" having all sorts of negative cultural baggage attached to it because of how some Christians misrepresent Jesus. How many people do you know who aren't Christians because they've never actually known a Christian who well-represented Jesus? Similarly, we all know a "feminist" who might be angry, filled with hatred toward men, and living in a victim mindset.

Just because the terms "feminism" or "Christianity" have some baggage attached to them doesn't mean we should avoid the pure and deep truths they represent. Christian feminism is simply this: the belief in the equality of men and women that follows the teachings of Jesus. It is the pursuit of the restoration of the original value of women, the perfect design that she can return to, now that Jesus has paid through his own life to remove the curse of the rulership of men once and for all time.

Since the fall, in every culture and society without exception, women have always been assigned a lower rank than men. It is the oldest, most pervasive form of discrimination and injustice in human history, and is so interwoven into culture that most of us don't even notice it.

Perhaps one of the most shocking attributes of Jesus' ministry on Earth was his counter-cultural attitude towards women. He didn't see or treat them as inferior in any way, which went radically against all the traditions of his day. We should not be surprised by this! Jesus was there in Genesis when God said, "Let us make man in our image, according to our likeness" (John chapter one also confirms Jesus' role in the creation of all things). Jesus did not value women according to the human cultural norms and standards that resulted from sin, he valued her according to her original created value.

Jesus had followers—who traveled with him—who were women. And some were not only followers, but financial supporters of his ministry! That would have been scandalous in his day.

Matthew, Mark, and Luke all record women following him during his time of ministry, and they all record women being present while Jesus was crucified and entombed, whereas Jesus' more numerous male followers are sparsely mentioned (only John is at the crucifixion). Mary Magdalene was also the first to discover the empty tomb on the third day, the first to speak to Jesus after his resurrection, and the first to bring the "good news" to the disciples that he had risen from the grave.

Beyond Jesus' women followers, he had several significant encounters with women that not only showed honor for them that was counter-cultural, but modeled his heart toward them.

The woman with the issue of blood (mentioned in Matthew, Mark and Luke) would have been considered ceremonially unclean in Jewish culture. If she had touched the garment of any Jewish Rabbi, it would have been considered not only offensive and unwelcome, but would have made him unclean as well. So when she touched the hem of Jesus' garment and he stopped everything to find out where his power went, she was afraid she was going to be in trouble, and fell to her knees. But Jesus didn't see her as unclean. Instead, he publicly commended her faith, which healed her.

Jesus' response to the woman caught in adultery recorded in John chapter eight would have been equally counter-Jewish culture. All the men were gathered around with rocks in their hands ready to stone her to death, as soon as Jesus gave the signal. Instead, when he asked if any of them were without sin (and whoever was could throw the first stone), they all dropped their stones and walked away. He pointed out that the men who accused her were no better than she was, not superior in any way. He showed her mercy, while the religious wanted to condemn her.

Perhaps my favorite recorded interaction Jesus had with a female was the woman who came in with a very expensive alabaster jar of perfume, and poured it over Jesus' head. The disciples tried to rebuke her for wasting something so precious, rather than selling it and giving the money to the poor, but Jesus praised her radical display of devotion to him. He even said, "I promise you that as this wonderful gospel spreads all over the world, the story of her lavish devotion to me will also be mentioned in memory of her" (Matthew 26:13, TPT). The disciples would have chosen religious activities, but Jesus said that a better choice was to honor him with everything we have of worth.

There is no record of Jesus ever behaving in any way that could be interpreted as an endorsement of assigning women a lesser value than men. In fact, all his interactions with women recognize them for their faith, devotion, and humility. Jesus made women famous who were wholly devoted to him. He would not agree with perspectives that perpetuated the curse of male rulership over women. It's not his nature. Even secular experts on the history of misogyny are perplexed by Jesus' counter-cultural attitude toward women.

Paul captured God's heart really well in Galatians 3:26-28 (NKJV):

> *"For you are all sons of God through faith in Christ Jesus. For as many of you as were baptized into Christ have put on Christ. There is neither Jew nor Greek, there is neither slave nor free, there is neither male nor female; for you are all one in Christ Jesus."*

If Jesus and those who were called by him did not draw hierarchies between men and women, why would we?

YOU DON'T HAVE TO PAY

Jesus is the answer to the curse of sin. He came to Earth willingly, knowing that his life would be the sacrifice that paid the price, once and for all. He came to restore what was lost in the garden. He came, as he said in Luke chapter four, to set at liberty those who were oppressed. And there has been no greater oppression seen in every age than the oppression of women, because it has affected roughly half of the world's population in various forms and fashions since the very beginning.

So why are so many Christian women stuck in places of captivity? Why is it so common for women to live a life of conforming, complying, and submitting to the rulership of men, when this was not her design? Why do so many women <u>choose</u> to stay captives? Some are captives in small ways, others in big ways, but the voluntary subservience of women is everywhere and extremely common.

We can come up with all sorts of great explanations including poor teaching (or more commonly a complete absence of teaching) in the church, a global lack of leaders modeling God's intended gender dynamics, and the epidemic of pride that often plagues men, resulting in control and manipulation. But I believe the greatest cause for women choosing captivity is the woman's own lack of self-value.

Now you're probably already cringing because you immediately associate self-value with pride. In fact, almost every woman I know has a hard time stepping into full alignment with God's value for her, for fear of becoming prideful and self-important. I believe this is the enemy's strategy— to keep women from understanding her value, by convincing her that it's prideful to seek a revelation of her own worth. It's not surprising that "Christian" leaders who are proponents of the inferiority of women frequently accuse women who step into their God-given anointings of operating in pride.

I'm convinced that if we as women could understand even a small glimpse of God's true value for us, we would never struggle in creating healthy boundaries and removing ourselves from abusive situations. If we really believed, "I was made in the very image of God, to co-rule and reign on Earth, and God has a plan for me, a plan to prosper me and not to harm me, a plan to give me a future and a hope," we would never find ourselves in captivity. If we believed in our true divinely assigned value, we would never be led away in deception where we become small and subservient.

This is why the devil's strategy to pile women down with religion and religious obligation has been so successful. If he can convince us that we are never good enough, that we must please, conform, and comply in order to be accepted by others, we will spend our entire lives down rabbit holes of performance that send us off trying to earn our value instead of stepping into the value already ascribed to us by God, a value that was worth Jesus giving his life to fully restore to us.

The great deception is: we have to pay to earn our way into God's favor, to be good enough. But the great truth is: before we even loved him, Jesus thought we were good enough, and he already paid to buy back our favor with God.

In the middle of my divorce from Kevin, my friend Lori had invited me to go to a conference called "Heaven Come." I was exhausted and didn't really have the emotional bandwidth or enthusiasm for a conference or a few days fighting traffic to L.A. and back—but Kevin "had the kids" that weekend, so I went with her.

I stood in the worship service, not feeling particularly connected to the song or the spiritual atmosphere. I felt overwhelmed by the things going on in my life. Truth be told, I was also feeling guilty for not being more present during worship, guilty for not being "spiritual enough" to not be overwhelmed by the Kevin drama, and overall felt I was just reaping the consequences of the choices I had sown in my life. I was not in a great frame of mind.

I closed my eyes, and I did what I always did when I didn't know how to pray: I prayed in the Spirit. Then I heard the voice of the Lord speak to me, saying: "You don't have to pay."

Consistent with how God always speaks to me, I knew it was him because it didn't make any rational sense at the moment. I was excited that I heard him speak! But what did he mean— I didn't have to pay for what?

The thing about hearing the voice of God is that sometimes the weight of his words is so significant that it can take years, or even a lifetime, to fully grasp its meaning. His mysteries are endless, and it's our joy and privilege to seek them out.

I'm not going to say I have yet fully grasped what it means that I don't have to pay, but I'm starting to see it. It means this: Jesus paid, in full, the entire price, for every mistake I would make, past, present, and future—he has already paid. The price of my sin was upon him, to bring about my peace and healing (see Isaiah 53).

I had been standing there in that worship service, with regrets, guilt, and shame, feeling like I deserved the pain I was in. But God didn't want me to live in that reality at all. The gospel means "good news" because it's the most tremendous news we would ever receive. He was asking me to take off the yoke of guilt and shame, and to take on his yoke, one that's easy and light. I don't have to pay, because Jesus already paid. This means: I was valuable enough for God's own son to pay for my life and return me to the garden. Like me, you've probably heard this a thousand times because it's such common language in our churches and our worship songs…but have you believed it? Do you actually believe that Jesus would have died if you were the only one to save? That is how valuable you are.

THE ENEMIES OF SELF-VALUE

Why do we as women lack value for ourselves? Sometimes it's because we confuse self-care with self-value. Self-care is definitely important. It says, "I take care of myself." Self-value is different. It says, "I value myself." You can't have self-value without self-care, but you can definitely have self-care without self-value.

One day on the phone, my friend Tami told me how God had been speaking to her about understanding her value. While she was talking, I thought smugly to myself, "This is not an issue for me, because I eat healthy, exercise regularly, enlist help when I need it at home and don't live like a martyr, I keep a good work-life balance, and I keep up with good, personal hygiene." But the next morning as I woke up, I heard the Lord say to me, "You don't value yourself." And while this was kind of a jarring revelation, it was kind of him to point out I was good at self-care, but actually believing in my own value was something totally different. He was inviting me into his heart to discover his value for me, so I could get aligned. Self-care is easy. It's outward and checks a box. Self-value is harder. It's inward and deep.

I realized this to be true: I would never achieve my potential in life if I didn't understand my own value and believe it. The same applies to you: unless you see and understand your true value, you won't achieve your potential in life either. More likely, you will live in a prison of serving someone else's expectations, because you've believed that was the "Christian" thing to do. But there is nothing Christian about sacrificing your own calling and destiny to defer to someone else. God made each one of us with a unique purpose. Only you can achieve what he has for you on Earth—you are an original.

There are three primary enemies of self-value: false humility, the trap of comparison, and deriving our value from humans and human structures.

Once I was at the gym with my personal trainer. We were having a conversation about her evening plans—she was going to go out to dinner with a girlfriend she hadn't seen since high school. My trainer was excited but also a little stressed about it. You see, her friend from high school had gained a lot of weight and looked a bit worse for wear. In a moment I will never forget, my trainer said, "I'm going to really go light on makeup and wear sweats or something, because I don't want to make her feel bad."

Something like a bolt of lightning hit me and I said, "You should never stay small on purpose to try to manage the insecurity of someone else." It was one of those moments when I knew what I said was so important, and so clearly from God, that I needed to go home and write it down right away. I realized I had never stepped into my own value while I was married to Kevin because I was really busy trying to stay small so I didn't make him insecure. This is the very definition of false humility. Having false humility means I suppress the expression of my identity to manage the envy, pride, and insecurity of someone else. It means I know that I'm big, but I pretend not to be, so someone else isn't bothered. This is a counterfeit form of humility, not the real thing. Self-value actually takes us out of false humility, not into pride.

The second enemy of self-value for women is the trap of comparison. We will never see our own value if we spend all our time looking at what everyone else has, what they look like, and wishing we had it, too. In the months following my divorce from Kevin, God really started talking to me about this. He took me to a scripture that knocked my socks off in Galatians 5:26b (TPT): "...for each of us is an original. We must forsake all jealousy that diminishes the value of others."

Jealousy actually diminishes the value of others, because it says, "I want what you have." It takes you out of your lane, and your own originality, and tries to move into someone else's lane and take their originality, and diminish their unique value. Hear this: you will <u>never</u> find your own value relative to another person. And envy, competition, and comparison will derail you from achieving God's unique plan for your life - guaranteed.

During my great awakening, before meeting Kevin, a well-known prophet came to my church, and he gave me a significant word about worship. He said that I was a rock-and-roller, not an "American Idol," but one made in God's image and his likeness. He said that God had given me a warrior sound in worship, but I was afraid of releasing it because I was afraid it would sound ugly—and because I compared myself with others. But God wanted to let a roar of a lion come out of me.

If you know any prophets, they'll tell you it's not usually a good sign if you get the exact same word from the same prophet a second time, because it means you've probably not stewarded the first word and taken action on it. A year later, this same prophet came back to my church and gave me almost exactly the same word. We laughed, because he said "I feel like I've only given this word to one person before," and I confirmed that it was me the year before. He said, "Daughter, I hear God say, stop comparing yourself to other people. I didn't create you like someone else, I created you like you. And there is a strength in your song, and you're afraid to let it out because it's the place where you think your voice sounds ugly, but it's the place where you're most anointed in worship." It was super hard for me to receive this word, because I wanted my voice to sound a certain way, like so-and-so, but God was telling me to cut it out, and to step into my anointing, which would only happen the way he uniquely made me to sing.

Comparing yourself to others isn't as innocent as it can sometimes seem; it's envy and jealousy. And where envy and self-seeking exist, confusion and every other evil thing are there (James 3:16). Envy opens the door to every evil, and it will keep us from stepping into our self-value and original design faster than any other deception.

Third and finally, we are kept from stepping into true self-value when we draw our worth and validation from humans and human structures. This happens when we seek the assurance, validation, and accolades of others, especially men, to tell us that we are valuable. Unfortunately, if your worth and validation come from humans and human structures, you will always serve them as your idols.

Speaking of human structures that become idols, I want to point out that rules and regulations established by human organizations and denominations that weren't directly from Jesus are religion. Religion sets criteria for acceptance that Jesus didn't set. We don't become righteous by following a set of rules, particularly rules created by humans. We become righteous through faith in Jesus alone. Check these out:

> *My passion is to be consumed with him and not clinging to my own "righteousness" based in keeping the written Law. My "righteousness" will be his, based on the faithfulness of Jesus Christ – the very righteousness that comes from God (Philippians 3:9, TPT).*

> *Nothing we did could ever earn this salvation, for it was the gracious gift from God that brought us to Christ! So no one will ever be able to boast, for salvation is never a reward for good works or human striving" (Ephesians 2:8b-9, TPT).*

Every single world religion, except the teachings of Jesus, introduces rules and regulations as the only way to succeed. The human condition, apart from Jesus, only understands "you get what you deserve." Hinduism teaches that your position in life was determined by your actions in your last life. Buddhism teaches you're only good enough to reach nirvana if you smother all your own desires. Islam teaches your outcomes are determined by your good works and religious devotion. Mormonism teaches that you get to Heaven through works-based righteousness. Even many Christian denominations create rules that aren't from Jesus: praying to people who aren't God, setting rigid rules on what people can or can't do, and establishing human hierarchies and power structures that give men power and control over others.

But for those who believe in Jesus, works that try to earn value, favor and acceptance from God are actually an affront to the cross. We must look to Jesus for our righteousness and nowhere else. If we focus on following rules to be accepted by God and others, we will never experience the freeing power of the cross. This doesn't mean that obedience isn't important—we must always obey God. But obedience without authentic connection to Jesus is dead works and dead religion. God doesn't want our outward circumcision, he wants the circumcision of our hearts (Romans 2:29).

Further applying these principles, we must also clearly recognize when women structure their lives around submitting under the rulership of men or under the rulership of religion that tells them to, this is a form of idolatry. Idolatry happens when we serve people or structures instead of God. It's no wonder women who live in these kinds of oppressive environments find it very challenging to connect with the Lord directly. It's as if God is asking, whom do you serve, them or me?

In case you're getting wrapped around the axle on what you think are scriptural requirements for a woman to submit to a man, I encourage you to read the entirety of Ephesians chapter five that deals with the role of a man and woman in marriage. The overwhelming conclusion from this important text is that the healthy model of a marriage is one of mutual submission and mutual devotion, not one where one party submits and the other rules. The healthy model is not when one party plays their Godly part as described in this chapter and the other doesn't. A marriage where one person rules and the other submits isn't God's model, it's abusive.

If you're still doubting, check out Jesus' teaching about what <u>his</u> style of leadership looks like:

> *Kings and those with great authority in this world rule oppressively over their subjects like tyrants. But this is not your calling. You will lead by a completely different model. The greatest one among you will live as the one who is called to serve others, because the greatest honor and authority is reserved for the one with the heart of a servant. For even the Son of Man did not come expecting to be served by everyone,*

but to serve everyone, and to give his life in exchange for the salvation of many (Matthew 20:25-28).

Jesus' model of leadership is rooted in serving, not ruling. When we see men "ruling" over women or even Christian religious structures that promote this kind of behavior, we need to remember these concepts didn't come from Jesus at all—who is not an advocate of ruling in relationships—but from the curse of the fall. Jesus' leadership style - for both men and for women - is to serve others. In relationships, men and women who serve one another both follow Jesus' definition of a leader.

STEPPING INTO SELF-VALUE

Women who fully understand what God believes about them will never find themselves captive to the enemy, because we cannot live in both captivity and freedom. So it becomes paramount for us to pursue a full understanding of how God values us. We do this through God's word, by pursuing prophecy, and by hearing God's voice for ourselves.

The primary way we pursue an understanding of God's value for us is from his word, the Bible. Perhaps like many Christians, you've been reading the Bible in a spirit of religious obligation, because you want to be good and not disappoint him. But I encourage you to stop your recurring read-the-Bible-in-a-year plan for a minute and ask God to use his word to speak to you, deeply. Try putting aside your task checklist and ask the Holy Spirit to come and breathe on his word. Religious obligation and the Spirit of God are not compatible. Read the word because it feeds your Spirit (Matthew 4:4 - man does not live on bread alone), and fills you with faith. Read it because it transforms you into the mirror of Jesus as you look at him (2 Corinthians 3:18). Read Song of Songs because you believe it is a love story about God and you. Read it until you believe it. God's word will always be a primary way he speaks to us. Heaven and Earth may pass away, but the word of the Lord stands forever (see Matthew 24:35).

A second important and Biblical way we understand our personal value and calling is through personal prophecy. God has always been speaking, and he didn't stop when the last of Jesus' apostles died. Jesus said in John 10:27 (NKJV), "My sheep hear my voice, and I know them, and they follow me." He wasn't just talking about followers in his day—but all those he came to save, in every generation to follow. Prophesy is a gift of the Holy Spirit, and it's the one Paul suggested we seek most of all. He said in I Corinthians 14:1, 3 (NKJV), "Pursue love, and desire spiritual gifts, but especially that you may prophesy…he who prophesies speaks edification and exhortation and comfort to men."

Prophesy is God's gift to strengthen, encourage, and comfort his people. Many Christians don't believe in prophecy because they've seen it abused or misused (or because they've been taught that the gifts of the Holy Spirit died in the Bible days…which ironically is not a Biblical conclusion at all). But just because some dysfunctional people have some erroneous views doesn't mean we should avoid this gift entirely. Speaking from my experience, I don't think I would have actually had the faith, courage, and strength to step out of captivity without the active role of Holy Spirit-inspired prophecies. I received my first word during my "great awakening" that God saw my humble heart and I didn't need to carry the shame of divorce with me, because like David said in Psalm 51, God never despises a contrite heart. I received a word that I was a delicate flower and that I had been in some wind and storms, but God was protecting me, and he was with me. I received a word that God was going to restore the foundation of my house (figuratively) and that I shouldn't give my house away, because it was God's gift to me (literally). I received a word that Kevin was frozen in a block of ice hanging outside my house and that God was giving me permission to choose what to do with him. I received words that God made my voice unique, because he made me unique, and that I didn't need to compare myself to others. Prophesy always encourages, and it's part of God's design for how his people are to be overcomers on Earth!

Another form of prophecy is when someone has an encouraging dream for us. One of the best prophetic dreams I've ever received was from my friend Lori. When I first told her I was getting divorced, she was not sure about it. She had seen first-hand how Kevin treated me, how he insulted me, marginalized my opinion, and limited my personal freedoms. However, her religious upbringing, like most Christians, seemed to summarize God's position on divorce as "God hates divorce" (which we now know is not the actual contextual meaning of Malachi chapter two).

So when I told Lori that I had decided to divorce Kevin, she was conflicted. She even told me, as an initial reaction, "Be prepared to go back to Kevin if God heals him." I wasn't on board with that at all. Now that I was free to choose, I was never going back to him. And I knew God would never ask me to, even if Kevin did get fully healed, because God is not a punisher. Rather than climb up on a religious soap box, Lori did what true Spirit-filled Christians should do in this kind of situation—she prayed. She asked God to show her his heart on the matter and how to be a friend to me. She asked to see the truth.

God answered by giving Lori a prophetic dream. In the dream, a demonic spirit was giving pills to women and convincing them to swallow them. Then he would ask them, pointing to a man, "Is that your husband?" And they would be confused, but answer yes. The enemy was giving women "roofies" and convincing them that someone was their husband.

When Lori told me about her dream, I wept. I wept because only a true friend would refrain from judging and instead seek the Lord in this situation. I wept because I tried to do the right thing and not live in self-justification or excuses for the mistake of marrying Kevin, but God had so kindly revealed in a dream to a close friend that I had actually been deceived by the enemy into marrying him. The enemy had "roofied" me. I was so encouraged by this prophetic dream.

Lastly, we step into our self-value by stewarding what God speaks to us directly. Learning to hear God is like learning to use a muscle for the first time. His voice never sounds like condemnation, and it never brings confusion. However, his wisdom is not our wisdom, so when he speaks, it might be so profound that it can take time to journey with him into the fullness of what he's saying. Nothing in my life has ever given me more joy, satisfaction, and identity than hearing God speak to me directly. And he is always speaking. We can hear him every day, if we want to.

The first time I really heard God, it was shortly after my "great awakening." I had traveled with my mom to a very exciting, very powerful, Holy-Spirit filled conference. I was pretty new to the Spirit-filled life, but I still knew when God was nudging me. My mom and I were really looking forward to the conference session where a famous missionary was speaking. She leads a ministry in Mozambique, Africa where she and her team have had a profound impact on the people, and they routinely see blind eyes opened, the dead raised, and the signs and wonders that Jesus promised would follow those who believe in him. I was really looking forward to her session. So I was surprised when I felt God nudging me to leave and go to the "soaking" room. I argued with him for a few minutes, but the pull was really strong.

I said, "Mom, I've gotta go."

"What? Right now?" She said, "She is about to come on!"

"I have to go to the soaking room. I'll meet you later."

I had seen conference signs with arrows pointing to where the "soaking room" was located, and I found it relatively empty. One man was laying on the ground snoring, it appeared his soaking had turned into a mid-conference nap.

I hadn't "soaked" before so I just laid down on the floor and relaxed. I knew God wanted me there, and I expected that He was going to show up.

I have no idea how long I was there, but this time of soaking at that conference is still one of the most significant encounters I've ever had with God.

I felt his presence come upon me. I felt a tremendous sense of peace. I knew he was extremely near. There was no better place to be, than there in the very company of the God of the universe. I felt all my striving fade away. All my anxiety I didn't know I was carrying melted away. I was still awake, but I lost all sense of time. I completely surrendered. My arms and legs became so heavy, it felt like I was attached to the floor. Then I heard him speak, and he said two things to me that would become pillars in my life.

He said, "The message is simple." And he said, "Isaiah 42."

When I was finally able to sit up, I grabbed my Bible and turned to Isaiah 42. I didn't remember ever reading it before, and there was no underlining or highlighting in that chapter of my Bible. I wept when I got to the end. I still weep every time I read this passage in verses 21-23 (TPT):

> *But this is a people plundered and robbed, trapped in holes and hidden in houses of bondage. They are like prey that no one will rescue, like spoil with no one to say, "Bring them back!" Doesn't anyone understand this? Will any of you pay attention to this in the future?*

When God spoke this to me, it was before I went into a decade of captivity married to Kevin. I didn't know I had been a captive to Henry and Mauricio, too. But God spoke something over me that was outside of time—he was inviting me to partner with him in my life's purpose to set free captives that no one else was rescuing. I didn't fully see it then, but the revelation of his words is not a one-time event.

I had also heard God speak to me "Isaiah 58," "Remove the Yoke," and "You won't walk through this alone" at the prayer service when I first woke up. I heard God say, "You don't have to pay" at the worship conference in L.A. And, I had also been hearing him speak to me frequently in the middle of the night. This is probably one of the easiest ways God can reach us, because all our defenses are down as we sleep. I had heard him say "Unless the Lord builds the house" (from Psalm 127), "There are spirits that oppose the seven Spirits of God" (see Isaiah 11:1-2), and "Resist the devil and he will flee from you" (see James 4:7). God's voice always reaffirms our value, and it always lines up with scripture.

THE VOICE OF THE STRANGER

If God is always speaking, and it's always to strengthen, encourage, and comfort us, we must also be aware that the devil is also always speaking, and it's always to drag us back into places of bondage and captivity. Lying is his native tongue, and he is a master of deception (John 8:44, TPT).

We must learn to discern when we are hearing the voice of God, and when we are hearing the voice of the accuser. Look at this from John 10:1-5 (TPT):

> *Jesus said to the Pharisees, "Listen to this eternal truth: The person who sneaks over the wall to enter the sheep pen, rather than coming through*

> *the gate, reveals himself as a thief coming to steal. But the true Shepherd walks right up to the gate, and because the gatekeeper knows who he is, he opens the gate to let him in. And the sheep recognize the voice of the true Shepherd, for he calls his own by name and leads them out, for they belong to him. And when he has brought out all his sheep, he walks ahead of them because they are familiar with his voice. But they will run away from strangers and never follow them because they know it's the voice of a stranger."*

Jesus desires mercy over sacrifice. The voice of the devil will try to keep us from mercy by quoting scriptures to us telling us we must sacrifice instead. Remember Psalm 51— the only sacrifice God really desires is a contrite and open heart, not the burnt offerings or any other effort-based sacrifice.

Jesus came to free the captives, and his voice will lead us to freedom. The voice of Jesus tells us that we have become righteous because <u>he</u> is righteous. Conversely, the voice of the enemy will try to convince us that our captivity is God's plan for our lives. The voice of the enemy will try to convince us that we can only become righteous through activities.

God says, "Rend your hearts, not your garments" (Joel 2:13a, NKJV). He means he desires our inward humility and openness to him, not our outward, performance-based sacrifices. The devil will try to convince us that the outward motions of Christianity is all there is to Jesus.

The devil comes, as the Pharisees did, accusing us of not adhering to the rules. This spirit of religious accusation murdered Jesus. May we always discern this spirit when it comes against us and not fall back into places of captivity dragging us into the fear of never being enough.

> *And you did not receive the "spirit of religious duty," leading you back into the fear of never being good enough. But you have received the "Spirit of full acceptance," enfolding you into the family of God. And you will never feel orphaned, for as he rises up within us, our spirits join him in saying the words of tender affection, "Beloved Father!" For the Holy Spirit makes God's fatherhood real to us as he whispers to*

our innermost being, "You are God's beloved child" (Romans 8:15-16, TPT)!

QUESTIONS FOR THE READER:

1. What negative associations of "Christianity" and "feminism" do you have that might be reflections of sources that may be misrepresenting God's truth?

2. If Jesus is the best example of the value and appropriate treatment of women, what do we learn from his life from scripture? What stands out most to you?

3. Are you living in any places of religious duty in your life where you are still trying to earn God's acceptance, when Jesus already paid?

4. Write down everything you currently think God believes about you. Do you think this is the complete picture? Read Psalm 139:17-18. Do you believe this?

5. Which of the enemies of self-value are present in your life? Which of the three ways to step into self-value do you plan to pursue more?

6. How can we discern the voice of God, compared to the voice of the enemy?

READ THIS PRAYER OUT LOUD:

Jesus, thank you that you were there in the beginning of all things, according to John chapter one. Thank you that you gave a perfect demonstration on Earth of the value you assign to women—the same value you assign to men. Thank you that you went against cultural norms and offended a lot of people to show us the right perspective on this. I ask that you would come with your Holy Spirit and show me any places where I choose sacrifice over mercy; where I'm trying to earn your acceptance in a trap of religious obligation, where I can simply receive what you have already paid for. Teach me to rend my heart and not my garments. Thank you,

God, that your good thoughts toward me outnumber the grains of sand on every seashore. I ask that you would come and gently lift away any veil of deception that is keeping me from aligning with the value you have for me. Show me how to value myself, to see myself the way you do. Thank you, God, that I recognize the voice of the Shepherd and that the voice of the stranger is easy to discern because it sounds strange. Thank you for giving me the gift of discernment of spirits so I might walk fully in truth.

Chapter Eleven

HIDDEN PAIN AND LEARNING TO FEEL AGAIN

God, I invite your searching gaze into my heart. Examine me through and through; find out everything that may be hidden within me. Put me to the test and sift through all my anxious cares. See if there is any path of pain I'm walking on, and lead me back to your glorious, everlasting ways - the path that brings me back to you.

Psalm 139:23-24 (TPT)

REMOVING THE RIND

The timing of finding my new church was amazing. I was getting to know so many incredible people who were authentic and not religious. They saw me and cared about me and prayed for me. I remember thinking that this must be what Jesus had in mind for his church.

In that healthy church and community atmosphere of God's presence, I could feel all my spiritual gifts that had been dormant for so long start to come back to life. I remembered how to partner with the Holy Spirit to pray for others. I began to play my keyboard and worship at home. Then I started to sing and play at church.

The church was pretty new and still small, and I got invited to a leadership retreat. I was so humbled and honored to be asked. I had been in Colombia for work meetings but landed and drove straight to the retreat, really excited to be there. I still could not believe I was able to make my own choices about where to go and what to do.

My church's lead pastors are very prophetic people. On the last night of the retreat, we worshiped and prayed for one another, and Pastor Mark gave me one of the most significant prophetic words I had ever received.

The word was that God was going to bring a redemptive ending to my story. And that God was going to seal up, like bookends, the hurts from previous seasons and relationships. And he saw that in twenty four months, I would be fully healed, and there would be a sweetness to my soul, and a readiness to my spirit, and God would make me ready for my next season of relationship and marriage.

Then he saw a picture of an orange. And he said, it's interesting that some fruit you can eat from the outside, but other fruit, like an orange or a grapefruit, has a rind. And the Holy Spirit showed him that like fruit with a rind, God had guarded the sweetness of my insides. Oranges can fall off the tree, they can be handled by many people, they can travel from one place to another and bump around the truck, but that exterior rind guards the integrity and sweetness of the fruit. And the Lord said he made me in such a way that I have this no-nonsense grace of leadership and authority on the outside, but it's always been a gift from God to protect the sweetness of my insides, and it was intentional, by design. But he heard the Lord say that he was peeling off the layer in this season. I had needed that rind for the past few years to guard the integrity and sweetness of my fruit, but the Lord was going to peel off that layer in the next twenty-four months, so I would be ready for my next season.

This word was extremely encouraging. Apart from the twenty-four months (which at the time seemed like an outrageously long time that it would take for me to fully heal), it was clear that God was doing an important work in me to remove the rind, and only then would I be ready for my redemptive ending— that included marriage.

"Removing the rind" is something I believe God must do for anyone who has woken up from a season of captivity. Humans can't survive ongoing emotional abuse without compartmentalizing all kinds of emotions in an effort to make it through each day. And I was grateful for the purpose my rind served for a season: it had kept me from being completely destroyed in my darkest night. But this was great news— God was removing the rind! I didn't need it anymore. I wasn't ever going back into a season where I needed it. I was free indeed.

I will give you a new heart and put a new spirit within you; I will take the heart of stone out of your flesh and give you a heart of flesh (Ezekiel 36:26, NKJV).

GOD WILL RESTORE ALL THE YEARS

God is so good to give gifts of prophecy to speak to us. At this point, I had been completely overwhelmed by how strengthened, encouraged, and comforted I was from the people who could hear the voice of the Lord and were getting words for me. But I had no idea how big of a word was coming next!

CHAPTER ELEVEN: HIDDEN PAIN AND LEARNING TO FEEL AGAIN

An amazing prophet came to my church, and he gave me a word. At this point, you may be thinking "Wow, how much prophesy is too much?" But I'm telling you, we should be living daily not on bread alone, but on every word that comes from God's mouth (Deuteronomy 8:3). God is always speaking, and each of us knows in part, and prophesies in part (1 Corinthians 13:9). We need the whole body of Christ for a full picture. I don't know about you, but I always want to be desperate to hear God's voice. I want to live every day on the fresh manna of his words.

I count this prophecy as one of the top three most important ones I've ever received. He said that he saw God ripping up a piece of paper and stomping on it, and that every covenant I had made that God didn't make—that God was stomping on it. He said that I felt overly-responsible for some things and it was like a handicap I felt, but God was releasing me from some things he never sent to me.

He said there was a twelve-year period stolen from me and God was going to restore all those years back to me.

He said what the devil thought would happen in the last three-and-a-half years, God stopped from happening because I put my trust in him. He said I had broken a curse of a lifetime of grief, hopelessness, and self-destructive behavior, because of my choice to trust God.

He said that my future was looking pretty great, that God had it all lined up.

I will never get used to the sheer power of God displayed when a perfect stranger who knows nothing about me receives information about me straight from Heaven. As much as I thought I had received freedom from the religious condemnation of getting divorced, I still felt significant relief that God was ripping up and stomping those covenants I had made, but HE hadn't made…that he was releasing me from the over-responsibility I felt for things (men) he didn't send me. It released me again from religious accusations. God didn't send me these men who tortured me. He was releasing me from feeling overly responsible for things not working out.

I had lost exactly a total of twelve years to Kevin-related captivity, and I believed what God said – that he would restore all the years.

And the crazy part was that three-and-a-half years prior was when I moved to California—and I had never been more isolated, depressed, alone, and self-medicating with alcohol. At that time, the enemy thought I would fully surrender to a life of control, isolation, manipulation, and self-destruction, but God rescued me because I trusted him. I remembered the dark night of the soul when I had lost all hope but decided to trust God anyway. All he required was my trust. And now, the curse had been broken. And my future was bright, God had it all lined up.

So I will restore to you the years that the swarming locust has eaten (Joel 2:25, NKJV).

SEE IF THERE'S ANY PATH OF PAIN I'M WALKING IN

My friend Tami convinced me to attend a special women's service at a nearby church. I wasn't super excited about going, but on nights when my kids were gone to their dad's house, it was still important for me to try to spend time connecting with others and not be alone in my silent, empty house. So I went.

At the end of the service, they invited everyone to come forward for prayer. I was anointed with oil, and I knelt at the altar and asked the Holy Spirit to come and touch me. I wasn't super faith-filled, or expecting much, so I was really surprised when I heard the voice of the Lord as I knelt at the altar that night.

He said, "Now it's time to give me all your hidden pain."

And then he said, "Then, I'm going to teach you to feel again."

True to how I always hear God, these statements were so out of nowhere that I knew it was his voice. Perhaps naively, I believed I had already given him my hidden pain, and I thought I did know how to feel. Apparently not.

I sobbed, letting his words sink in. And I asked him to show me how to do it: how to give him my hidden pain and how to learn to feel. Part of me was afraid to feel—because I was afraid of the pain that might also come. But I was determined, like Pastor Mark had prophesied, to allow the Lord to peel the exterior orange "rind" away—to put off the protective shell and be ready for my next season of life.

CHAPTER ELEVEN: HIDDEN PAIN AND LEARNING TO FEEL AGAIN

A specific scripture kept repeating itself in my heart over and over from Psalm 139:24 (TPT): "See if there is any path of pain I'm walking on." I invited him to show me "paths of pain" I still walked in, and he did. I didn't want any hidden pain to stay hidden— I knew he could only heal what I brought to him in the light.

I had spent so many years stuffing my pain away, it was going to be a bit of a process to pull the painful memories out, to bring them to the light, and to ask the Lord to come and heal me. And each time I did, it was like he was pulling out the poison from my memories, and their power to continue to cause pain was removed. It seemed so simple, but it was a blessed relief. I was going to give him everything, nothing held back or hidden. He was making my heart whole again. It wasn't a fast process, and it certainly wasn't easy, but it was worth it.

God had been speaking to me through the story of Hannah from First Samuel. Hannah was one of two wives of Elkanah, and she was his favorite, even though she was barren and without children. Elkanah's other wife was horrible to Hannah, provoking her year after year because of her barrenness, making her weep and suffer.

To me, the best part about this story was that Hannah didn't hide her feelings from God. She didn't put on a brave face, try not to make a scene, pretend to be okay, and silently suffer, so no one would be bothered. No, Hannah went to the tabernacle of the Lord, with all her bitterness and all her anguish, and wept before God, pouring out her heart before him. After hearing her explanation for her behavior and realizing the depth of Hannah's lament was not from drunkenness but from intense and real heart sorrow, the priest Eli blessed her.

God heard and remembered Hannah. And she had a son and dedicated him to God. Her prayer in First Samuel chapter two is one of my favorite prayers in the Bible because of the raw emotion and gratefulness of Hannah's rescue and her declarations about who God is.

I was reminded of the importance of not hiding our feelings from God. Sometimes religion tells us that we should not approach God honestly because he's some aloof, detached tyrant that doesn't have time for our everyday troubles. Or even worse, religion tells us to minimize the honesty in our cries to God because "if we were better, we wouldn't feel afraid, or alone, or scared, or helpless or in need." I think this is one of the enemy's strategies to keep us separate from God. And for someone who had just spent endless years pretending to be okay, it wasn't yet natural for me to be real with God, or anyone else. But he was inviting me to hold nothing back—to bring the whole ugly mess to his feet, and see what beauty he would give in exchange for ashes.

As I gave my hidden pain to God, I realized that opening my heart to him and sharing my feelings with him was not going to be a one-time process, but a new, open-hearted way of living - forever. If he was a mean or vindictive God, I would not be able to do it. But he is kind and offers us a light burden, and he is a safe place. When we live a life of honesty before God, where we constantly bring him our wounds, we allow him to continually heal and refresh us, so that the enemy does not gain a stronghold in our hearts.

FORGIVENESS

I woke up one morning to the Lord's Prayer playing like a tape in my head. When it got to the part about forgiving others, I felt like God was underlining it: "Forgive us our debts, as we forgive our debtors" (Matthew 6:12, NKJV).

I knew that forgiving Kevin was going to be the only thing that fully released me from him. I knew forgiveness was something God required. I also knew that harboring even a small amount of unforgiveness wouldn't punish Kevin, but would just poison me instead. God had delivered me from believing Kevin was one hundred percent bad, and that was important. But forgiving him was a different process.

I started simply by saying out loud, "I choose to forgive Kevin." I repeated it every time I needed to, which was every day for a while. Each time, it got easier to say. Then I felt like I needed to take it a step further and say out loud, "I bless the father of my children." This one was harder. I didn't really feel like blessing him, but I knew this had to happen for me to be free. Blessing him didn't mean I was going to pretend like he didn't harm me, but it meant I wanted him to be healed by God and not stay in his own captivity. I prayed and released my need for vengeance. Vengeance belongs to the Lord.

There are a lot of different kinds of forgiveness journeys. Some are about forgiving one-time events, or forgiving someone for causing wounding who is no longer alive. But my journey was about forgiving someone who still fired darts at me. The cruel and condescending behavior hadn't stopped, it was ongoing. Kevin was still the father of my children, and he wasn't going away.

I asked God to show me his heart for Kevin, because I mostly still saw him as a despicable, depraved, hostile piece of work. And it was pretty hard to see what God showed me. He showed me that he loved Kevin, that he created him with a purpose, that his desire was for him to be whole and free, that even he wasn't beyond God's kindness and restoration—if he chose it. If he humbled himself, God would wash him totally clean and forgive all his debts, just as God had forgiven me.

There is a significant lightness that comes when we fully let go and forgive. When I did, it severed the last unhealthy tie I had to Kevin. It didn't mean I would pretend not to be upset when he misbehaved in the future, but it did mean that I would do my part not to engage in angry responses but to choose to forgive, again, seventy times seven (see Matthew 18:22).

QUESTIONS FOR THE READER:

1. Have you been living with a protective rind around your heart, keeping pain out, but also keeping you from being able to authentically connect with the Lord and with others? Why do you think God didn't remove my rind until I was fully out of captivity?

2. Are there covenants you have made that God did not make? Is he trying to release you from feeling overly responsible for outcomes in relationships that he may have never sent to you?

3. What paths of pain are you walking in? How do we bring our hidden pain to the Lord? Do you need to ask the Lord to take you by the hand and teach you how to feel again?

4. When we live in unforgiveness, how does it keep us attached to the person we haven't forgiven? What does Jesus' model prayer in Matthew 6:12-15 teach us about forgiveness?

READ THIS PRAYER OUT LOUD:

Jesus, thank you for making me perfectly, for knowing everything I would need to overcome the enemy. Thank you for protecting my heart with a rind, for keeping me from complete destruction, and for guarding the integrity of my fruit. Thank you for taking me by the hand and walking me all the way out of my captivity, and into the fullness of freedom from the curse and religious obligation. Thank you that you don't keep me bound in covenants you didn't make or relationships you didn't send me. Thank you that you give endless second chances to your children whom you love, who come before you in humility. Thank you for healing my heart, for removing my heart of stone, and giving me a heart of flesh, according to your word. Thank you for showing me all the places of hidden pain I'm walking in that you want me to surrender to you, so you can make me whole. Thank you, Jesus, for removing my rind and teaching me how to feel again. I choose to forgive everyone who has wounded me, even if they aren't sorry. I release them now, and I release my need to punish them. I give them fully over to you, God, and I thank you that you forgive me because I forgive others.

CONCLUSION

Then I heard a triumphant voice in heaven, proclaiming: "Now salvation and power are set in place, and the kingdom reign of our God and the ruling authority of his Anointed One are established. For the accuser of our brothers and sisters, who relentlessly accused them day and night before our God, has now been defeated - cast out once and for all! They conquered him completely through the blood of the Lamb and the word of his testimony. They triumphed because they did not love and cling to their own lives, even when faced with death. So rejoice, you heavens, and every heavenly being! But woe to the earth and the sea, for the devil has come down to you with great fury, because he knows his time is short."

Revelation 12:10-12 (TPT)

APPLY THE BLOOD: THE POWER OF CHOICE

Just because Jesus paid the full price to reverse the curse of sin in the garden doesn't mean it automatically applies. If it did, we would all be back in the garden, completely naked, without any sickness or sin, enjoying full intimacy with God, with full intimacy restored between all men and women. No, our choices play a role in returning to the garden—our choices and our faith.

The blood of Jesus already paid the price, but the blood must be applied. The veil was already torn in half from top to bottom at the moment Jesus died on the cross, but we must walk through the torn veil to find reconnection with the Father and our original inheritance on the other side.

Sin and the curse did a lot more than create a catastrophic rift of inequality and rulership between men and women. It's also what introduced sickness, disease, short life spans, the requirement to toil and labor to produce fruit from the ground, the increased difficulty in childbirth, and ultimately the fact that humans would be born into sin—born into separation from God.

That is why Jesus said we must be born again. We were all born into sin and the curse, but we can be born again—born of the Spirit of God (see John 3). When we are born again, we have complete access to break the power of the curse. This is why Jesus told us that those who believed in him would do everything he had done on Earth, including healing the sick and raising the dead (John 14:12). Our restored inheritance is not only to be fully freed from the curse ourselves, but to now free others.

I know it's radical, but I believe in difficulty-free childbirth because Jesus broke the curse. I believe it's God's will to physically heal every person who comes to him, because Jesus paid for it, and because Jesus healed every person who came to him in scripture. This is one of the toughest areas of tension of true Christianity, because not everyone with faith ends up with a difficulty-free childbirth, and not every person we pray for is healed. But I refuse to lower the bar for what Jesus wants to do on Earth to the level of my own personal experience. If he came to break the curse and restore us to our original position in the garden, we should not stop pursuing him short of that reality.

When it comes to women who live in the curse of captivity of the rulership, abuse, manipulation, and control of others, I believe it is the heart of God to free each and every one. This could look like both the woman and the man in a relationship waking up and getting fully restored. It also might look like the woman choosing to leave her abusive marriage because God values freedom over adherence to religious rules. But to apply the blood of Jesus and to exit captivity is always a matter of our choices.

Choice led to the fall, and choice leads to redemption. By choice, men separated from God through sin and the curse was the result. Now by choice, we accept the gift of Jesus, to restore all that was lost. But choice is the key. God never wanted robots who didn't have choices. Love can only exist where there is choice. Without choice, we don't have love. Instead, we have religion, control, and manipulation. Many will not choose him, but love always offers a choice.

In Luke 10, when Martha complained to Jesus that her sister Mary wasn't helping with the house chores, Jesus surprised everyone by pointing out Mary had made a better choice—to sit at his feet, and that it would not be taken from her. I think sometimes we live in a "Martha mindset" thinking that all the obligatory church things are the priority when Jesus wants us to choose connection with him instead. We might be surprised how often we are faced with a choice between religious duty and drawing closer to Jesus. While we will always be able to choose, as Jesus said, there is always a better choice. It doesn't look like religion, and it will not be taken away from those who choose it.

The biggest lie I ever believed was that I had no choices, and I must stay in slavery. Religion can do that to a person—bind us up, believing we must conform and comply and be good and not disrupt the status quo. I thought

I was choosing righteousness, but the reality was, I was choosing captivity. There is always a choice.

Jesus came to liberate the oppressed—and if we choose to take his hand, believe in the power of his blood, and walk through the veil, he will return us to the garden. It might not look like what we thought, and it will require great faith and risk, but no cost of freedom is too high. Only in freedom from captivity can we walk in closeness with God, sitting at the feet of Jesus, to whatever destiny he has prepared for us. Only by walking with him in the garden do we find true peace, true joy, and true fulfillment. We consider everything else a loss compared to the greatness of knowing him intimately (Philippians 3:8-9). It can be scary leaving the captivity of Egypt. What will we eat? Where will we live? What is ahead? But I promise you, there is no greater relief than leaving the pain and torment of oppression behind and stepping into a season of supernatural peace and stillness in our hearts.

THE SECOND DREAM AND JOSEPH

The dream I had of the drowning woman before I woke up was the most vivid dream I'd ever had. But then I had a second dream, and it was just as vivid—and I knew it was just as important.

In my dream, I'm lying in bed with Kevin. It's strange because I'm on the side of the bed he would sleep on, and he's on my side. I'm sure it's Kevin, but then his face changes to Henry. Somehow I'm in bed with both Kevin and Henry. Or better said, I'm in bed with whatever they both represent to me.

In my dream, I know I need to get out of there. I know I have a choice, but I am so afraid of leaving. I am not sure what exactly I'm afraid of, but the fear is powerful. It has kept me frozen there for a very long time. I am paralyzed with fear.

I lay there for what seems like forever, gathering my resolve. I am so afraid of what Kevin/Henry will do to me if I get out of that bed. Finally, I act. I sweep the covers aside and stand up. I say to myself, "I'm leaving, I can't stay here any longer."

Smirking, Kevin/Henry jumps out of bed to confront me and transforms into a woman. She has long, greasy, stringy, red hair and is hideous-looking. She is in my face. She sneers at me, saying "Oh really? You will <u>never</u> leave." She's intimidating for sure, and I know she's a demonic spirit. It seems like she's been around in my life for a long time. And she is completely sure I won't leave, because I never have before. But I already made my choice. I am not afraid anymore.

I look at her for a moment, then I say, "I'm leaving" and I step around her to get in the shower. I don't look back and she doesn't follow.

And in my shower (in my dream), I heard the Holy Spirit clearly say:

"If you wouldn't have gotten out of that bed and been healed, you would never have been able to see and heal this wound in others."

I never aspired to be a writer. I also never wanted to be a poster child for the biblical equality of women, overcoming emotional abuse or getting free from the control of a narcissist. But this one thing I do know: God does not waste anything. And the place where the enemy wounds us—the place where we must personally overcome the most darkness—will always become the place where we gain the greatest spiritual authority in helping others to overcome.

Remember Joseph. He dreamed that he would become great, and his envious brothers sold him into slavery and left him for dead. Then he was falsely accused and imprisoned. It seemed like God had abandoned him. But he didn't give up or die in prison. He sought God to interpret some dreams that eventually landed him in the palace and the top job besides Pharaoh. When his brothers bowed down and repented for what they had done, Joseph said one of my favorite things in all of scripture in Genesis 50:20 (NKJV):

> *"But as for you, you meant evil against me; but God meant it for good, in order to bring it about as it is this day, to save many people alive. Now therefore, do not be afraid; I will provide for you and your little ones." And he comforted them and spoke kindly to them.*

When the brothers of Joseph humbled themselves and apologized, he didn't bash them over the head with their mistakes. He comforted them.

Perhaps, for those who make a choice to step out of the deception of the curse, our response should be similar. God never despises a contrite heart. And what the enemy meant for harm, God meant for good.

A CALL TO THE CHURCH OF JESUS

All of creation is waiting for the revelation of God's sons and daughters (see Romans 8:19). Many sons have been honored and revealed across the ages. But what of the revelation of God's daughters? Made in God's image, the woman is a mighty rescuer, a threat to the powers of darkness that blanket the Earth. Woman is the second half of God's people, those to whom Jesus has given his very own authority (Luke 10:19).

The church must not simply tolerate the woman, but must tear down the misogynistic structures that have sometimes subtly and sometimes overtly pushed the co-carriers of God's own image underneath a hierarchy of power and control that was never God's design. God made women as co-heirs of the Earth, to co-reign with man. She reflects God's very nature, as does man. The equality of men and women is God's perfect design. Man is one hundred percent man, and woman is one hundred percent woman, and both man and woman reflect God's image one hundred percent.

These hierarchical structures, the result of the curse, run deep and wide in our societies, in many of our church bylaws, in the hearts of our leaders, pastors and boards of deacons, and in the minds of our young men and women who grow up believing this is the way of things. We have unwittingly endorsed cultural norms that peg women as inferior and have thus prevented her from taking her seat with Christ in heavenly places. But just because the curse has become normalized in our society and in our belief systems, does not mean that it's God's plan or his way. Jesus came to break the curse of sin—every part.

This subject matter has become more complicated than it needs to be. As I said earlier, either God made men and women as equals, or he didn't. If we believed, based on Genesis chapter one, in the equality of the sexes, we would stop tolerating even the seemingly most innocent patterns of thinking that keep women in places of subservience. We would stop permitting discussion of unilateral submission requirements, notions that appoint the man as spiritual leader of the home (effectively asserting that a woman cannot lead spiritually in the home alongside the man), and any other hierarchical structure that can be traced back to the curse. These are the kind of commonplace misalignments with God's word that have kept millions of women trapped in abusive situations since the beginning of time.

Remember when Jesus' disciples were upset because a certain village didn't receive him? They were so offended, they asked Jesus if they should call down fire to burn up those who didn't honor him. And Jesus famously rebuked them and said, "You don't know what manner of spirit you are of." I believe the same applies to those who vehemently defend their positions that women should not preach, should not be pastors, or even more subtle rulership philosophies that believe she is less-than. I wonder what Jesus would say about "what manner of spirit" they are operating in. To me it feels like pride, envy, control, manipulation, fear, religious obligation, the same spirit that kept me in oppression for years, and well…the curse.

For some, what's needed is a minor adjustment in thinking. For others, it will be a bigger process that will require humility, repentance, and breaking agreement with powerful demonic forces. But Jesus did not condemn the woman in adultery, nor does he condemn any who humble themselves. This is not an invitation to throw rocks at those who aren't on the same page with women's equality, but it is an invitation for all to discover God's heart on this issue and to come into alignment with his design and his plan, so the end-times church can fully mobilize. It's an invitation to shed the layers of cultural norms and what we might have grown up hearing and seeing, and an invitation to look to Jesus for his unfiltered view of his design for women.

Eventually, Jesus is going to return to Earth for his bride, the church. And when he does, the church will have made herself ready (Revelation 19:7). Jesus is not going to return when half the bride has not been made ready. God's sons and daughters must both be ready.

I can hear the Spirit of God whispering, "Daughters, wake up, and return to the garden." It's time. And believe me—all of hell is trembling at their approach.

# EPILOGUE

A dear friend at church had a dream about me. In her dream, I was at Disneyland. On my left, I was holding the hand of my oldest son, and he was holding the hand of my youngest son. On my right, I was holding the hand of a man, and he was holding the hand of a little girl.

In the dream, we approached a grassy area. The man knelt down to the little girl and asked her for permission for me to marry him. The little girl was overjoyed and enthusiastically answered yes.

Then the man approached me, and pulled out a large oval diamond ring, and asked me to marry him. I said yes.

When my friend told me about the dream, at first I wondered if the little girl was the daughter of the man, but my friend didn't believe so. She had a strong sense that the little girl was me as a child, and that God wanted to return me to a place of childhood innocence and original hopes and dreams for marriage. Disneyland represented the place where dreams come true, of pure joy and magic. And it was important that childhood Rebecca be consulted in this marriage decision—childhood Rebecca who believed that marriage could be sweet and tender, and that men were not all selfish takers.

Over the years I had lost, buried, and smothered all my expectations for marriage. The only way to not be constantly disappointed was to stop expecting things. But God wanted to renew my little-girl dreams for marriage. He wanted to remove the rind of my old season fully. He wanted to restore all that was lost. So I opened up another chamber of my heart to him, the place of ruined romantic hopes, and asked him to come and make it new.

A few months later, I was having dinner with Jean, my friend who had the hummingbird stuck in her kitchen. She was catching me up on her life, and I was catching her up on mine—everything amazing that God was doing and saying.

At the end of dinner, Jean looked me in the face with an expression that means, "God just spoke to me," and she said, "I know you are going to marry someone who has never been married before. And the reason I know this is because you have never actually been married before either."

This hit me so hard it was like all the air got sucked out of the room. But she was right—nothing I had experienced so far had anything to do with how God actually designed marriage. God was raising my hopes and expectations for the future, and it was pretty exciting. And the twenty-four months of healing that had been prophesied was almost over. A new season was coming, and it was going to look totally different. Because God makes all things new.

> *Because you received a double dose of shame and dishonor, you will inherit a double portion of endless joy and everlasting bliss!*
>
> (Isaiah 61:7, TPT)

ABOUT THE AUTHOR:

Rebecca is a follower of Jesus, a business executive, a mom of two energetic boys and was recently married to a wonderful man from Boise. In her 20-year business career, she has led business lines that generated a few hundred million dollars of annual revenue, was recognized in Fortune's 40 Under 40, and has traveled all over the world leading strategic projects. Her kingdom pursuits include a love for God's presence (wherever it can be found) and serving on the worship team and prayer team at her home church Oceans Church in Orange County, California. Her loves include walks in the hills, any opportunity for karaoke, and when someone else cooks.

Connect with Rebecca